CW01549921

SARVEPALLI RADHAKRISHNAN (1888-1975) is widely recognized as modern India's greatest philosopher. He was also a statesman of distinction, and is compared to Plato's ideal of the philosopher-king.

As a creative thinker and a distinguished interpreter of Indian thought, he philosophized in the true Indian tradition. His notion of religion was spiritual, and not institutional or denominational.

Born in the pilgrim soil of Thiruttani, Tamil Nadu, he was deeply influenced by India's rich vedic tradition in his formative years. Starting with his first teaching appointment in the Department of Philosophy at Madras Presidency College in 1909, he quickly established his reputation, and soon became George V Professor of Philosophy in Calcutta University and, in 1936, Spalding Professor Eastern Religion and Ethics at Oxford University.

In 1952 he accepted the office of India's first Vice President, and in 1962 assumed the office of the President of India.

He was knighted in 1931 and conferred the *Bharat Ratna* Award in 1954.

By the same author
in
Orient Paperbacks

Adaptive Indian: Identity and Ethos
Foundation of Civilisation: Ideas and Ideals
Indian Religious Thought
Religion, Science and Culture

Turning Dreams *into* Reality
LIVING WITH A PURPOSE

S. Radhakrishnan

Orient Paperbacks
DELHI | MUMBAI | HYDERABAD

ISBN : 978-81-222-0624-1

Living With a Purpose: Turning Dreams into Reality

Subject: Biographies / Essays

© S. Gopal

1st Published 1977
This edition 2020

Published by
Orient Paperbacks
(A division of Vision Books Pvt. Ltd.)
5A/8 Ansari Road, New Delhi-110 002
www.orientpaperbacks.com

Printed and bound at Thomson Press, New Delhi

CONTENTS

1.	Kalidasa	9
2.	Guru Nanak	29
3.	Swami Dayanand Saraswati	37
4.	Raja Rammohan Roy	42
5.	Acharya Jagdis Bose	46
6.	Gopal Krishna Gokhale	55
7.	Bal Gangadhar Tilak	67
8.	Motilal Nehru	73
9.	Lala Lajpat Rai	83
10.	Rabindranath Tagore	91
11.	Sardar Vallabhbhai Patel	108
12.	Dr. Rajendra Prasad	118
13.	Acharya Shri Tulsi	127
14.	Maulana Abul Kalam Azad	137

Key for Diacritical Marks

The truly great are not the men of wealth, of possessions, not men who gain name and fame, but those who testify to the truth in them and refuse to compromise whatever be the cost. They are determined to do what they consider to be right. We may punish their bodies, refuse them comforts, but we cannot buy their souls, we cannot break their spirits. Such men deserve our admiration.

S. Radhakrishnan

India's spirit,
grace and genius.

ONE

Kalidasa

(4th – 5th Century CE)

Great classics of literature spring from profound depths in human experience. They come to us who live centuries later, in vastly different conditions, as the voice of our own experience. They release echoes within ourselves of what we never suspected was there. The deeper one goes into one's own experience, facing destiny, fighting fate, or enjoying love, the more does one's experience have in common with the experiences of others, in climes and ages. The most unique is the most universal. The Dialogues of the Buddha or of Plato, the dramas of Sophocles, the plays of Shakespeare, are both national and universal. The more profoundly they are rooted in historical traditions, the more uniquely do they know themselves and elicit powerful responses from others. There is a timeless and spaceless quality about great classics.

Kālidāsa is the great representative of India's spirit, grace and genius. The Indian national consciousness is the base from which his works grow. Kālidāsa has absorbed India's cultural heritage, made it his own, enriched it, given it universal scope and significance. Its spiritual directions, its intellectual amplitude, its artistic expressions, its political forms and economic arrangements, all find utterance in fresh, vital, shining phrases. We find in his works simple dignity of language, precision of phrase, classical taste, cultivated judgment, intense poetic sensibility and fusion of thought and feeling.

In his dramas we find pathos, power, beauty, and great skill in the construction of plot and delineation of character. He is at home in royal courts and on mountain tops, in happy homes and forest hermitages. He has a balanced outlook which enables him to deal sympathetically with men of high and low degree, fishermen, courtesans, servants. These great qualities make his works belong to the literature of the world. Humanity recognizes itself in them though they deal with Indian themes.

In India Kālidāsa is recognized as the greatest poet and dramatist in Sanskrit literature. While once the poets were being counted, Kālidāsa as being the first occupied the last or the little finger. But the ring-finger remained true to its name, *anamika*, nameless, since the second to Kālidāsa has not yet been found. Tradition associates Kālidāsa with King Vikramaditya of Ujjayini, who founded the Vikrama era of 57 B.C. The change in the name of the hero of *Vikramōrvaśīya* from Pururavas to Vikrama lends support to the view that Kālidāsa belonged to the court of King Vikramaditya of Ujjayini. Agnimitra who is the hero of the drama *Mālavikāgnimitra* was not a well-known monarch to deserve special notice by Kālidāsa. He belonged to the second century B.C. and his capital was Vidiśā . Kālidāsa's selection of this episode and his reference to Vidiśā as the famous capital of a King in *Meghadūta* suggest that Kālidāsa was a contemporary of Agnimitra. It is clear that Kālidāsa flourished after Agnimitra (150 B.C.) and before A.D. 634, the date of the famous Aihole inscription which refers to Kālidāsa as a great poet. If the suggestion that some verses of Mandas or inscription of A.D. 473 assume knowledge of Kālidāsa's writings is accepted, then his date cannot be later than the end of the fourth century A.D. There are similarities between Aśvaghoṣa's *Buddhaçarita* and Kālidāsa's works. If Aśvaghoṣa is the debtor, then Kālidāsa was of an earlier date than the first century A.D. If Kālidāsa is the debtor, then his date would be later than the first century.

It is suggested that Kālidāsa belongs to the Gupta period (A.D. 320-547) and lived in the reign of Chandragupta II, who had the title of Vikramaditya. He came to power about A.D. 345 and ruled till about A.D. 414. Whichever date we adopt, we are in the region of reasonable conjecture and nothing more.

Kālidāsa speaks very little of himself and we cannot therefore be sure of his authorship of many works attributed to him. There is, however, general agreement about Kālidāsa's authorship of the following works:

1. *Abhijñāna-Śākuntala*, a drama in seven acts dealing with the love and marriage of Duṣyanta and Śākuntala;
2. *Vikramōrvaśīya*, a drama in five acts dealing with the love and marriage of Pururavas and Urvaśi;
3. *Mālavikāgnimitra*, a drama in five acts dealing with the love of Mālavika and Agnimitra;
4. *Raghuvaṃśa*, an epic poem of nineteen cantos describing the lives of the Kings of the solar race;
5. *Kumārasambhava*, also an epic poem, of seventeen cantos, dealing with the marriage of Śiva and Pārvatī and the birth of Kumāra, the lord of war;

6. *Meghadūta*, a poem of 111 stanzas[1] describing the message of a Yakṣa to his wife, to be conveyed through a cloud;
7. *Ṛtu-Saṃhāra*, a descriptive account of the six seasons.

Kālidāsa takes up his themes from the traditional lore of the country and transforms them to achieve his object. For example, in the epic story Śākuntala was a calculating, worldly young woman and Duṣyanta a selfish lover. The poet wishes to exhibit the sentiment of love from its first awakening in a hermitage girl, to its fullest perfection through the stages of separation, frustration, etc. In his own words, a play must present the diversity of life, and communicate charm and sweetness to men of varied tastes:

Traiguṇyodbhavam atra loka-caritaṃ nānārastaṃ
dṛśyate nāṭyaṃ bhinna-ruçer janasya bahudhāpy ekaṃ
samārādhanam.

We do not know any details about Kālidāsa's life. Numerous legends have gathered round his name which have no historical value. From his writings it is clear that he lived in an age of polished elegance and leisure, was greatly attached to the arts of song and dance, drawing and painting, was acquainted with the sciences of the day, versed in law and learned in the philosophical systems and ritual practices. He travelled widely in India and seems to have been familiar with the geography of the country from the Himalayas to Kanya Kumari. His graphic description of the Himalayan scenes, of the saffron flower — the plant of which grows in Kashmir, look like those of one who has personal acquaintance.

The master artist suggests, by a few touches, what others fail to express even by elaborate discourses. Kālidāsa is famous for his economy of words and naturalness of speech in which sound and sense match. His pen-pictures are graceful and perfect, the royal chariot in full speed,[2] the running deer,[3] Urvaśi's bursting into tears,[4] Narad's appearance in the sky like a moving *kalpa-vṛkṣ*.[5] He is master in the use of simile and analogy.

Sarasijam anuvidham saivalenapi ramyam
malinam api himansor laksma laksmim tanoti
iyam adhika-manojrid valkalenapi tanvi
kim iva hi madhuranam mandanam nakirtinam.

'A lotus, though intertwined with moss, is charming. The speck, though dark, heightens the beauty of the moon. This slim one, even with the bark dress, is more lovely. For what is not an embellishment of lovely forms?'[6]

Kālidāsa's writings instruct not by direct teaching, but by gentle persuasion as by a loving wife. Mammata says: *kāntāsammitatayopadeśayuje; ramadivat vartitavyam, na ravanadivat*. By an aesthetic presentation of great ideals, the artist leads us to an acceptance of the same. We live vicariously the life of every character that is set before us, and out of it all comes a large measure of understanding of mankind in general. Kālidāsa projects his rich and glowing personality on a great cultural tradition and gives utterance to its ideals of salvation, order, love. He expresses the desires, the urges, the hopes, the dreams, the successes and the failures of man in his struggle to make himself at home in the world. India has stood for a whole, integrated life and resisted any fragmentation of it. The poet describes the psychological conflicts that divide the soul and helps us to pull the whole pattern together.

Kālidāsa's works preserve for us moments of beauty, incidents of courage, acts of sacrifice and fleeting moods of the human heart. His works will continue to be read for that indefinable illumination about the human predicament which is the work of a great poet. Many of his lines have become almost like proverbs in Sanskrit. *Kumārasambhava* opens with a verse in which the poet speaks as if the Himalayas were the measuring rod spanning the wide land from the east to the western sea.

He suggests that the culture developed in the Himalayan regions may be the 'measuring rod' of the cultures of the world. This culture is essentially spiritual in quality. We are ordinarily imprisoned in the wheel of time, in historicity and so are restricted to the narrow limits of existence. Our aim should be to lift ourselves out of our entanglement, to an awareness of the real, which is behind and beyond all time and history, that which does not become, that which is absolute, non-historical being itself. We cannot think it, enclose it within categories, images and verbal structures.

We know more than we can think and express it in historical forms. The end of man is to become aware by experience of this absolute reality. Compare the words of *Raghuvaṃśa: 'brahmabhūyam gatiṃ ājagama.'* The man of enlightenment reaches the supreme timeless life. The performer of good deeds has heaven for his share. We know the Real by the deepest part of our being: *ātmānam ātmanā vetsi.*[7] The Real is the knower and the known: *vedyam ça veditā çāsi.*[8] Again: *yaṃ akṣaram veda-vido vidús tam ātmānam atmany avalokayantam.*[9] The Supreme leads a life of contemplation. Though he grants the fruits of others' austerities, he himself performs austerities: *svayaṃ vidhātā tāpasaḥ phalānām kenāpi kāmena tāpaś çaçāra.*[10]

The Absolute which is the Real beyond all darkness is superior to the division of spirit and matter. It is omniscient, omnipresent and almighty. It manifests itself in the three forms (*trimūrti*), Brahma, Vishnu and Śiva — the maker, the preserver and the destroyer. These gods are of equal rank and a believer may select any form which appeals to him for worship. In daily life, Kālidāsa was a follower of the *Śaiva system.*[11] The opening invocations of the three dramas *Śākuntala, Vikramōrvaśīya, Mālavikāgnimitra*, show that Kālidāsa was a devotee of Śiva.

The opening verse of *Raghuvaṃśa* reads:

vāgarthāviva saṃpṛktau vāgartha-pratipattaye jagataḥ
pitarau vande pārvatī-parameśvarau.

While in *Mālavikāgnimitra*, the Lord should set us on the right path, *saṃmārga*, in *Vikramōrvaśīya*, he is said to be easily attainable by devotion, *bhakti-yoga-sulabha*, in *Śākuntala*, the Lord in his eight-fold form is seen. Immediate insight into the Divine reality is the aim of religion.

Though Kālidāsa worshipped the Divine as Śiva, his attitude was not in any way exclusive or narrow-minded. He had the catholic attitude of traditional Hinduism.[12] He treated with great respect the views of others.

Kālidāsa has sympathy with all forms of religion and is free from prejudice and fanaticism. Each person can tread the path which appeals to him, for the different forms of Godhead are the manifestations of the One Supreme who is the Formless behind all forms.

tvameva havyaṃ hotā ca bhojyaṃ bhoktā ca śāśvataḥ
vedyam ca vedītā cāsu dhyāta dhyeyaṁ ca yatparam.[13]

Raghu, after installing Aja on the throne, retires to the forest, takes to a life of meditation and attains that which is beyond darkness.

tamasah paramapadavyayam purusam
yogasamadhina raghuch.[14]

Until the end of religion, the realization of the Supreme, the ascent from the vanity of time is attained, we will have opportunities for making progress towards the goal. In this journey towards the end we will be governed by the law of karma. Kālidāsa accepts the theory of rebirth.

ramyāṇi vīkṣya madhurāṃś ca niśamya śabdān
paryutsukī bhavati yat sukhito'pi jantuḥ
tac cetasā samarati nūnam abodha pūrvam
bhāva sthirāṇi jananântara sauhṛadāni.

Sita, when banished by Rama, says:

When he is born, I'll scorn my queenly station
Gaze on the sun, and live a hell on earth,
That I may know no pain of separation
From you, my husband, in another birth.[15]

This life is one stage in the path to perfection. Even as the present life is the result of our past deeds, we can shape our future by our efforts in this life. The world is under a moral government. The good will ultimately triumph. If we have no tragedies in Kālidāsa, it is because he affirms the ultimate reality of concord and decency. Subject to this conviction, he induces our sympathy for the hard lot of the majority of men and women.

Kālidāsa's writings dispose of the misconception that the Hindu mind was attentive to transcendental matters, and neglectful of mundane affairs. Kālidāsa's range of experience was wide. He enjoyed life, people, pictures and flowers. He does not separate men from the cosmos and from the forces of religion. He knows the full range of human sorrow and desire, meagre joy and endless hope. He points to a harmony of four main interests of human life, *dharma, artha, kāma* and *mokṣa*, the ethical, the economic, the artistic and the spiritual. The economic including the political and the artistic should be controlled by ethical norms. Ends and means are bound together. Life becomes livable only through valid ties. To cleanse and illuminate those ties was the poet's task.

Kālidāsa did not feel called upon to choose between religion and morality on the one side and progress and security on the other. These are not hostile to each other.

History is not a natural but a moral phenomenon. It is not a mere temporal succession. Its essence lies in the spiritual which informs the succession. The historian should penetrate and comprehend that inward moral dynamism. History is the work of man's ethical will, of which liberty and creativity are the expressions.

The kings of the Raghu race were pure from birth, ruled over extensive domains stretching from earth to the ocean, *asamudra ksitisanam*. They amassed riches for charity, spoke measured words for the sake of truth, were eager for victory for the sake of glory, and were householders for the sake of offspring. They gained knowledge in childhood, enjoyed the pleasures of life in youth, adopted the ascetic life in old age and in the end cast away their bodies by yoga or meditation.

The kings collected revenues for the prosperity of their subjects, *prajānam eva bhūtyartham*, even as the sun takes up water to give it back a thousand fold. The rulers must stand up for dharma, justice. The king is the real father of the people, he educates them, protects them and provides for their livelihood, while the actual parents are only the causes of their physical birth.

Everyone in Aja's kingdom thought that he was a personal friend of the king.

ahameva mato mahī-pateriti sarvaḥ prakṛitiṣvacintayat.

The ascetic tells the king in *Śākuntala*: 'Your weapon is for the protection of the afflicted and not for striking at the innocent', *ārta-trāṇāya vah śastram na prahartum anāgasi.* Bharata, the son of Duṣyanta and Śākuntala, from whom this country takes its name is called *sarvadamana* — not merely one who conquered every ferocious beast of the forest but has achieved self-control also. Self-control is essential for rulership.[16]

In *Raghuvaṃśa*, Agnivarna gives himself to dissipation. He has so many mistresses that he cannot always call them by their right names. He develops a wasting disease and as, even in that condition he is unable to resist the pleasures of the senses, he dies.

Kālidāsa gives us pictures of the saint and the sage, the hero and the heroine with their nobility. They are the directing minds within a civilization. Nobility and self-control are their distinctive characteristics. Discipline is essential for a decent human life. Kālidāsa says: 'Even though produced in a mine, a gem is not worthy of being set in gold, O noble lady, so long as it is uncut.'

apyakara samutpanna mani-jatir asamskrta
jata-rupena kalyani na hi samyogam arhati.[17]

Though Kālidāsa's works exalt austerity and adore saints and sages, he does not worship the begging bowl.

The laws of dharma are not static and unchanging. The tradition of the past has to be interpreted by one's own insight and awareness. Tradition and individual experience interpenetrate. We are the inheritors of the past but are also trustees of the future. In the last analysis, each one must find the guide for one's conduct in the innermost centre of himself. When Arjuna, in the opening chapter of the *Bhagavadgītā*, declines to conform to the demands of society which impose on him as a kṣatriya the obligation to fight; when Socrates says, 'Men of Athens, I will obey God rather than you'; they are taking their stand on inward integrity rather than on outward conformity.

In early Vedic literature the unity of all life, animate and inanimate, is indicated and many of the Vedic deities are personifications of striking aspects of nature. The idea of retreat into nature, a mountain top or a forest hermitage, in search of the revelation of the spirit of the universe, has been with us from early times. As human beings we have our roots in nature and participate in its life in many ways. The rhythm of night and day, changes of seasons suggest man's changing moods, variety and capriciousness. Nature had not become mechanical and impersonal for Kālidāsa. It had still its enchantment. His characters have a sensitive appreciation of plants and trees, of hills and rivers and a feeling of brotherhood for animals. We see in his writings flowers which bloom, birds which soar and animals which spring. We find a striking description of the love of the cow in *Raghuvaṃśa*. The *Ṛtu-Saṃhāra* gives a moving account of the six seasons. It reveals not only Kālidāsa's vision of nature's beauty but also an understanding of human moods and desires.

In *Śākuntala* when the curtain rises, Śākuntala and her two friends are seen watering the plants, creepers and trees of Kanva's hermitage, where the stars and colours in the sky, the pretty flowers and the lively animals are vital parts of human experience. Śākuntala does not look upon nurturing the plants as a drudgery, but finds joy in it.

na kevalam tata-niyogah asti mamapi sodarasneha etesu.

'Not merely because my father has ordered it, I also have fraternal affection for them.'

For Kālidāsa rivers, mountains, forests, trees possess a conscious individuality as animals, men and gods.

Śākuntala is a child of nature. When she was abandoned by her *amānuṣi* mother Menaka, the birds of the sky pick her up and rear her until the sage Kanva takes her under his fostering care. Śākuntala tended the plants, watched them grow and bloom and the occasions when they burst into blossoms and bore flowers and fruits were celebrated as festive days. Like a loving mother Śākuntala reared up her pet animals and plants. No wonder they responded. On the occasions of Śākuntala's wedding, trees sent their gifts, forest deities showered their blessings and cuckoos cooed aloud their joy. The hermitage was filled with grief at the prospect of Śākuntala's departure. The deer drop their mouthfuls, the peacocks stop their dancing and the creepers shed their leafy tears.

When Sita is cast away, the peacocks abruptly stop their dance, the trees shed off flowers, and the female deer throw away the half-chewed *darbha* grass from their mouths:

nrtyam mayurah kusumani
vrkasah darbhanupattan vijahur harinyah
tasyah prapanne sama-dhukha-bhavam
atyantam asid ruditam vane'pi.[18]

Kālidāsa takes up an object and creates it for the eye. He had a strong visualizing power. Look at the vivid description of the flight of the antelope which Duṣyanta pursues to the hermitage:

grīvbhangābhirāmam muhur anupatati
syandane datta-drṣṭih
paścārdhena praviṣṭah śarapatanabhayād
bhūyasā pūrvakāyam
darbhair dhāvalīdhaih śamavivṛta
mukhabhraṁśibhih kīrṇa-vartmā
paśyodagraplutatvādviyati bahutaram
stokamurvyām prāyati.

'His glance fixed on the chariot, ever and anon he leaps up peacefully bending his neck; through fear of the arrow's fall he draws ever his hinder part into the front of his body; he strews his path with the grass, half chewed, which drops from his mouth opened in weariness; so much aloft he bounds that he runs rather in the air than on earth.'

Kālidāsa's knowledge of nature was not only accurate but sympathetic. His observation was wedded to imagination. His descriptions of the snows of the Himalayas, of the music of the mighty current of the Ganga, of the different animals, illustrate his human heart and appreciation of natural beauty.

No man can reach his full stature until he realizes the dignity and worth of life that is not human. We must develop sympathy with all forms of life. The world is not made only for man.

The love of man and woman attracted Kālidāsa and he lavished all his rich imagination in the description of the different kind of love. He does not suffer from any inhibitions. His women have a greater appeal than his men, for they reveal a timeless universal quality, whereas the men are dull and variable. They live on the surface while the women suffer from the depths. The competitiveness and self-assertion of the men may be useful in the office, factory, or battlefield, but do not make for refinement, charm and serenity. The women keep the tradition alive with their love for order and harmony.

When Kālidāsa describes feminine beauty, he adopts the conventional account and falls into the danger of sensuous engrossment and sometimes over-elaboration. In *Meghadūta* the *Yakṣa* gives a description of his wife to the cloud:

tanvi śyāmā śikhari-daśanā pakva-bimbādharọṣṭhī,
madhye kṣāmā, cakiṭa-harini-prekśana, nimnanabhih,
śroni-bharat alasa-gamana, stoka-namrā-stanabhyam,
ya tatra syad yuvati-visaye srstir adyeva dhatuh.

'There she lives who is, as it were, the first creation of Brahma amongst women, slim, youthful (or fair in complexion), with pointed teeth, a lower lip red like a ripe bimba fruit, thin at the waist, with her eyes like those of a frightened female deer, with a deep navel, slow in gait on account of heavy hips and bending a little low by the weight of her breasts.'

See also the King's description of Mālavika in II:

dirghaksam sarad-indu-kanti-vadanam bahu
natavamsayoh samksiptam nibidonnata-stanam urah
parsve pramrste iva madhyah panimitomitam ca
jaghanam pada-varalanguli chando nartayitur yathaiva
manasi slistam tathasya vapuh.

'Her face has long eyes and the lustre of the autumnal moon, the arms slope down by the shoulders. Her chest is compact with thick and swelling breasts; her sides are (smooth) as though planed off. Her waist is measurable by the palm of the hand and her hips are broad and the feet have curved toes, and her body is fashioned to suit exactly the fancy of the mind of a dancing master.'

He gives us here a pen-picture of a typical dancing girl which may well make a painter envious.

In the gallery of women Kālidāsa presents, we have many interesting types. For many of them the conventional pretences and defences of society did not work. Their conflicts and tensions called for integration. Their men felt certain and were secure. They accepted polygamy as the normal rule. But Kālidāsa's women had imagination and understanding and so were victims of doubt and indecision. As a rule they were not fickle but trustful, sincere and loving.

Love is deepened by hardships and sufferings borne for the sake of love. It grows a hundred-fold in its intensity by obstacles to its realization, even as the current of a river blocked on its way by uneven rocks (flows with greater force). Even in the absence of fulfilment, the yearning gives all the joy that love means. The pathos of separation finds poignant expression in *Meghadūta*, in *Rati-vilapa* and in *Aja-vilapa*.

Happiness of love in union is found in *Vikramōrvaśīya*.

In *Mālavikāgnimitra* the queen is called Dharini because she bears everything. She has dignity and forbearance. When Mālavika attracts the notice of the King in a dance scene which the clown has contrived, she rebukes the King in words of harsh satire, that such efficiency would be of advantage if shown in affairs of the state: *yadi rajakaryesv api idrsi upaya-nipunatarya-putrasya tatah sobhanam bhavet*. When her husband's affection shifted to Iravati and then to Mālavika, her devotion to him persists. The *parivrājikā* Kauśikī observes: 'These noble women attached to their lords, serve them even though it be against their own desires.'

By a series of misfortunes, Kauśikī is led to the religious life. She comforts and distracts the minds of Dhāriṇī. Though a nun, she is an authority on the dance and the cure for snake bite.

Irāvatī is passionate, impetuous, suspicious, demanding and dictatorial. When she was abandoned in favour of Mālavika by the King, she bitterly complains and rebukes the King in harsh words.

Agnimitra's love for Mālavika is of the sensual type. The King is fascinated by the beauty and grace of the maid. In *Vikramōrvaśīya* we have a blend of the human and super human. Urvaśi's character is somewhat removed from normal life. She has power to watch her lover unseen and overhear his conversations. She is lacking in maternal affection, for she abandons her child rather than lose her husband. Her love is selfish and her transformation is the direct outcome of a fit of insane jealousy.

Pururavas sings in rapturous terms of love and says that the sovereignty of the world is not as sweet, as blissful, as the lover's labour at the feet of the beloved. The world is dark and desolate to whom love is denied but it is bright and blissful to love triumphant.

In this play we have the development of blossom into fruit, of earth into heaven, of passion based on physical attraction into love based on moral beauty and spiritual understanding. Śākuntala inherits from her mother Menakā, beauty and lightheartedness, and from her father Viśvāmitra, the famous ascetic, patient and forgiving love. Freedom of sense and austerity of life brought her into being. In her own life the two, freedom and restraint, earth and heaven combine.

In the first Act we find all the impulsiveness of youth. The daughter of the hermitage in the first outburst of passion gave herself away in simple innocence and complete trust to the King. She followed the unsuspecting path of nature as she had not learned to control her feelings and regulate her life by norms.

Duṣyanta through forgetfulness, for which the poet does not make him responsible, does not recognize her. He says that he should not look at another's wife, *anirvarnaniyam parakalatram*. Śākuntala suffered the worst that could happen to a devoted wife: she is disowned by her husband and disgraced. Her mind becomes vacant and she stands there lonely, filled with terror, anguish and despair. The poet narrates her endurance of desertion, her fortitude in suffering, her later disciplined life till she is restored to her husband. Love is not a mere affair of the senses; it is kinship of spirit. Both Duṣyanta and Śākuntala suffered, were disciplined by sorrow, and obtained the reward of a spiritual harmony. The youthful flush subsides; the gust of passion dies out. Love is won at a higher level and the brief glow of pleasure is turned into a steady life of bliss. Passion is linked with the sanctities of life. Nature and grace blend in harmony.

Kālidāsa does not judge the first union of lovers as a moral lapse. They are not sinners but they have to grow through suffering.

Love born of sense attraction should be transformed into love based on austerity and control. While striving to reach heaven, both Pārvatī and Śākuntala had to skirt the edge of the abyss.

Sex life is not inconsistent with spiritual attainment. Wild life or unrestrained passion is inconsistent with it. Sex life under law and restraint is spiritual in character. One can lead the life of a householder and yet be a hermit in temper. The *Upaniṣad* says: Enjoy by renunciation, *tyaktena bhuñjîthā.*

The goal of life is joy, serenity, and not pleasure or happiness. Joy is the fulfilment of one's nature as a human being. We must affirm our being against the whole world, if need be. When Socrates was condemned to death or when Jesus was crucified, they did not take death as defeat but as fulfilment of their ideals. The aim of love is a happy harmony of man and woman. The concept of *ardhanārīśvara* brings it out. The wife does not belong to the husband but makes a whole with him.

The wife is the root of all social welfare.

kriyānām khalu dharmyānām satpatnyo mūlasādhanam

The wife is the *saha-dharma-cāriṇī.*

iyān corvasi yāvad āyus tava saha-dharma-cāriṇī bhavatu.

She is with him in the performance of all his duties. Indumati was to Aja a housewife, a wise counsellor, a good friend, a confidante and a beloved pupil in learning the fine arts.

gṛhiṇī sacivaḥ sakhi mithaḥ priya-siśyā lalite kalā-vidhau.

Kālidāsa believes that marriage is fulfiled in parenthood. The physical attraction is sublimated through suffering caused by misunderstanding, separation, desertion, cruelty, etc. and attains its fulfilment in the child. The marriage of Śiva and Pārvatī was brought about for the birth of Kumāra. This country is named after Bharata, son of Duṣyanta and Śākuntala. In *Raghuvaṃśa*, it is said that the love of Dilīpa and Sudakṣiṇa increased when it was shared by the love of the son also.

rathanganamnor iva bhava-bandhanam babhuva
yat prema parasparasrayam
vibhaktam apy eka-sutena tat tayoh parasparasyopari
paryaciyata.[19]

In *Raghuvaṃśa*, III. 23, Kālidāsa says that Dilīpa and Sudakṣiṇa rejoiced in the birth of their son even as Uma and Śiva were gratified by the birth of Kārttikeya, as Saci and Indra by the birth of Jayanta.[20] The marriage of Duṣyanta and Śākuntala found its fulfilment in the birth of their son Bharata. The birth of Kumāra was the main aim of the marriage of Śiva and Pārvatī. Kālidāsa loves children, as is evident from his descriptions of Bharata, Āyus, Raghu and Kumāra.

For Kālidāsa the path of wisdom lies in the harmonious pursuit of the different aims of life and the development of an integral personality. He impresses on our mind these ideals, by the magic of his poetry, the richness of his imagination, his profound knowledge of human nature and his delicate descriptions of its most tender emotions. We can apply to him the words of Miranda in *The Tempest*.

> *O wonder,*
> *How many goodly creatures are there here!*
> *How beauteous mankind is! O brave new world,*
> *That has such people in't.*

References

[1] Some MSS have a few additional verses.

[2] *Vikramōrvaśīya*, 1.4.

[3] *Abhijñāna-Śākuntala*, 1.7.

[4] *Vikramōrvaśīya*, V.15.

[5] *Ibid.*, Y. 19.

[6] *Abhijñāna-Śākuntala*, I.17.

[7] *Kumārasambhava*, II,10; see *Bhagvadgīta*, X.15.

[8] *Kumārasambhava*, II.15; see *Bhagvadgīta*, XI.17.

[9] III.50.

[10] I.57.

[11] The cult of Śiva worshippers developed around eleventh century.

[12] Yuan Chwang tells us that, at the great festival of Prayaga, King Harśa dedicated a stature to the Budha on the first day; to the Sun, the favourite deity of his father, on the second; and to Śiva, on the third.

[13] *Kumārasambhava*, II.4, 15.

[14] *Raghuvaṃśa*, VIII, 24.

[15] *Raghuvaṃśa*, XIV. Ryder's English translation. He refers to the child in her womb.

[16] Kautilya remarks: *bharata iti lokasya bharanāt*. He is called Bharata because he supports the world. VII.33.

[17] *Mālavikāgnimitra*, V., 18.

[18] *Raghuvaṃśa*, XIV.

[19] *Raghuvaṃśa*, III, 24.

[20] *umd Vnsankau sara janmand yatha, yatha jayantena sacipurandarau tatha nrpah sa ca sutena magadhi nanandatus tat samau.*

One earth, one family.
Goodwill to the whole of humanity.

TWO

Guru Nanak

(April 15, 1469 – Sep 22, 1539)

Our country's history has witnessed periods of glory and gloom, triumph and tragedy, victory and defeat. Whenever we passed through gloomy periods a prophet arose to call us back to the truth, telling us how we had deviated, how in our actual life we had disregarded the teachings of the great seers.

Nanak was born in a period of crisis — not political and social, but moral and spiritual. People were lost in the observance of trivialities, the celebration of ceremonial piety and the acceptance of meaningless dogmas, which kept people away from one another, which separated them, instead of bringing them together. It was an age of social chaos which was repugnant to the heart of any right-thinking man. Guru Nanak, therefore emphasized what may be regarded as the central principles of any true religion — inward vigilance and outward efficiency. These are the things on which he laid the greatest stress.

Nanak emphasized on *Oṃkāra*. That is all that he believed in, but what is *Oṃkāra*? If you try to find out what *Oṃkāra* means, it is a composite of the three: 'a' 'u' 'ma' (*ākāra, ukāra, makāra*): 'a' stands for the waking state, 'u' stands for the dreaming state, and 'ma' for *suṣupti*. All the three taken together, sublimated into one, is *pranava* or *Oṃkāra*.

Oṃkāra gives you comprehensive reality. It includes the waking, dreaming and dreamless states of human consciousness. There is no other state of human consciousness. All these are, therefore, merged into one Absolute Reality. Guru Nanak did not quarrel about dogmas because *Oṃkāra* has been said to be invisible, qualityless, unexperienceable — *shivam, shāntam, advaitam*. This is the one fundamental reality, truth is the highest, *satnam*. God is truth, and there is nothing higher than truth.

Nanak also said that if one wished to understand what this truth is, it is essential for him to enter into the secret chamber of his heart. God is not to be found in the sky above, or in the stars there or in the waters here. He is to be found in the deepest part of man's being. It is that man who is truly religious who is God-intoxicated, who is God-possessed, who has seen into the meaning of existence. It is such people who are regarded as religious in our country, not those who mutter *japas*, or go to shrines or temples. They may be on the pathway to the Divine, but the man who realizes God is one who sees the Divine in his inmost being.

There is a secret dwelling place in each man's heart, where the Divine is to be felt, is to be touched and experienced. This is what we should do. Prayers, meditations and spiritual exercises are all methods which are devices for helping us to know the deepest in us. This is what the purpose of all true religion is.

This does not mean that we should retire into monasteries or go to mountain tops, lacerate our bodies, torture our minds and give up the world. People who do so are not truly religious. Men who neglect their duties and merely utter the name, Krishna, Krishna, are the enemies of God; ignorant people who do not know what Reality is. For the sake of humanity, God himself has taken birth in this world. If He has done that, is it not our duty to express our deepest convictions in our daily life and in our national behaviour?

The time has come when we have to accept Guru Nanak's teachings that names do not matter, that the pathways do not matter. The man who has seen God is truly religious, not those who talk about God and lead atheistic lives. The authentically religious man will never do a thing that is repugnant to his conscience, or that is unholy in any sense of the term.

Guru Nanak told us about *satnam*, the practice of good conduct, the leading of a good life. That is the highest test; *satnam* is great, but greater than that is the practice of love, the practice of compassion. That is what he told us. We talk big and practise little. We all constitute the body of God, and anybody who breaks that body, tears it asunder, is an enemy of God.

Are we not doing it every day of our lives? Are we not disintegrating the human being? Are we not breaking this human body into pieces and thus crucifying God Himself? That is what we are doing day after day.

It is, therefore, necessary for us not merely to remind ourselves of the great teachings of Guru Nanak, *satnam* and *sadachara*, but ask ourselves every moment of our lives whether we are really practicing the great teachings that we profess. If we do practice them we will never have these social discriminations, we will never have religious differences. We may start with austerity; austerity will lead to tolerance; tolerance will lead to respect and we will respect what other people hold sacred. Such should be the attitude of a truly religious soul.

If you have hatred in your heart, if you have ignorance in your mind, if there is superstition in the dark spaces of your heart, take it from me that you are not a religious man but pretending to be a religious man. A truly religious man will be filled with light, joy and compassion for the whole of humanity.

At a time, when most of us are attached to the things of the world which is becoming increasingly stale and mechanical, becoming intellectualized and secularized, it is good to remember that we have another dimension to our existence and if that is not fulfilled, our life itself is incomplete. Lives of prophets, like Nanak, are an inspiration and a rebuke. An inspiration because they make us feel that there is a side to our existence, a spiritual dimension, which we generally overlook. That is why most of the people in this world today are restless, quarrelling about little things and not realizing that there is the light of lights in each one, *jyotisam jyotih*. It is there in every human being. We overlook it. Because of our overlooking it, we are alienated from our internal being. We live on the surface, but do not get into the depths of our own lives. Most of us lead such outward lives.

Guru Nanak drew our attention at a time when we were forgetting the realities of the world, that there is something pure, changeless, timeless, which persists for all times; he told us about the original rock from which we are hewn, the original spring from which we all derive our existence.

Nanak rebukes us because we have forgotten our own true nature. We live on the surface; we lead superficial lives.

Guru Nanak told us about *satnam*, the practice of good conduct, the leading of a good life. That is the highest test; *satnam* is great, but greater than that is the practice of love, the practice of compassion. That is what he told us.

Religious life does not mean a life which is withdrawn from the world. Many people think that the lives of saints have a certain grimness and gloom. This is not true. Those who live in God do not take a harsh view of the misfits or the failures of society, and have full compassion for and full understanding of all the ills to which a human being is subject. They understand the vicissitudes through which we pass, the chances and changes; why we trip, why we fall into temptation. So sanctity is not unworldiness; it is a frame of mind, an attitude from which we look at all the things in this world. That is a thing which we all recognize.

The greatest prophets are those who are found feeding the hungry, healing the sick and excusing the sinner. That is the work which they do. We must, therefore, understand that sanctity or holiness is not unworldliness, it is participation in the agony of the world with a proper frame of mind that there is a Supreme Power which can be depended upon and which never fails us.

The other lesson which Nanak taught us is the common ground which subsists between many of our religions. In his time he was faced by antagonism of Hindus and Muslims and he said, 'Why are you quarrelling about forms, about ceremonies, about dogmas, about sacred places, etc. Like this you will find that everyone is worshipping the same Supreme; we are all pilgrims in the same quest. We are all trying to find out where God is, how we can reach him.' That is the lesson which he taught us. There is a common ground between the religions of the world. In his time, Nanak took up Hindus and Muslims and he taught them that the *Quran* and the *Puranas* teach the same thing; whether it is a mosque or a temple, we see the same God. Nanak's rebuke we still deserve because we are still leading superficial lives. We are not truly religious; we are not caught into the depths of our consciousness and do not realize the Supreme who is there. The same Supreme dwells in every human being and if we are quarrelling among ourselves we are crucifying the Lord. The Lord is crucified and His body is torn to pieces. It is necessary for us to understand in this age of mingling of cultures, of religions, etc., that there is a common substratum from which all religions spring. They are the varied expressions of the one and the same Reality. So, there is a spiritual dimension. That sanctity is not withdrawal from the world, that all religions preach the same gospel, and those who are quarrelling about them are not truly religious, these are some of the lessons which Nanak taught us.

It is well known that all great arts centre round religious leaders: music, painting, sculpture, literature, all these centre round and get inspiration from the great religious leaders. Great teachers do teach us these things; they ask us to abolish caste, get rid of untouchability, etc., but it takes a long time for us to practice those teachings. We still suffer from these disabilities. Guru Nanak himself repudiated them and asked to repudiate them. But we are still practicing them in our lives. We are theoretical believers in Guru Nanak's teachings. Practically, we are giving the lie to the teachings which he gave us. It is, therefore, necessary for us to institute a kind of self-scrutiny and try to wage an inner war, so to say, against false inclinations and appetites from which we all suffer.

We have had with us, from the beginning of history, people who told us, 'One earth, one family. Goodwill to the whole of humanity,' how many of us have really borne testimony to those great truths in our actual lives? We know today that violence is much more common than it used to be. Why is it that we are unable to adhere to the teachings which these great sages and saints have given to us?

Religion is not a thing which you can buy or get from going to a temple, church or gurdwara. It is a thing which you can practise only if you wage incessant war on the baser instincts, which still have so much command over human nature. These are the things which we have to set aside if we wish to be true followers of any great sage or teacher.

The great teachers asked us to become new beings. Have we ever attempted to become new in our character, in our outlook? We are always trying to practise religion with our spinal cord, repeating mantras or chanting hymns and thinking that we are religious. But a truly religious man is not made that way. He institutes a different kind of being in his own nature. It is that new being that constituted the greatness of Guru Nanak Dev and it is that thing which we have to bear in mind when we try to adopt his teachings. Caste, untouchability, religious differences — Hindu, Muslim, Sikh, etc., all these things he asked us to set aside and he asked us to remember that we all belong to the one household of God.

A social reformer, a crusading zeal,
a powerful intellect.

THREE

Swami Dayanand Saraswati

(Feb 12, 1824 – Oct 30, 1883)

Among the makers of modern India, the chief place will be assigned to Swami Dayanand Saraswati. At a time when there was spiritual confusion in our country, when many of our social practices were in the melting pot, when we were overcome by superstition and obscurantism, this great soul came forward with staunch devotion to truth and a passion for social equality and enthusiasm, and worked for the emancipation of our country in all its dimensions — religious, political, social and cultural.

~

To take the first aspect, the religious one: he was guided by the rule of reason. We have a number of sayings of his to this effect: some people worship the waters, the Ganga and so on, others worship the stars, still others worship images made of clay and stone; but to the wise man the Supreme dwells in his own heart, in his own soul.

The Supreme is to be found in the inmost depths of the human being. The culture of our country accommodated every possible way of approaching the Divine, and so it gave a place to image worship also.

The supreme place was given to the practice of the presence of God. To get at it, we have to practise *dhyāna* and dharma. But many people are not able to concentrate their minds on the Supreme. Still others are of a nomadic character who cannot be brought even to that stage. Some idea of God must be given to them by any means that one can possibly have, but all the time one's emphasis must be on the oneness of God.

The *Vedas* tell us: of all the Gods, the Supreme original Godhead is one and there cannot be any multiplicity of gods.

When we talk of the great souls and *avatārs*, we must realize that they are the manifestations of the one Supreme. There is only one Supreme Deity in this world. He may appear in varied forms but do not mistake the shadows for the substance. The Substance is One and Supreme and all our attention must centre round that Reality of which all these are to be regarded as different kinds of manifestation.

~

This existence of Godhead is not regarded as merely a speculation, or a dogma, or something which you derive from the prophet's words or the sage's words. It is something which you have to acquire by pursuing the rule of reason. Swami Dayanand Saraswati was one who was guided by the supremacy of reason and he made out that the *Vedic* scriptures never asked us to take anything on trust but to examine everything and then come to any kind of conclusion.

We are called upon to find out what the Ultimate Reality is. A father tells his son that from which all things are derived, that by which they are sustained, that into which they are dissolved, that is supposed to be the Supreme Reality.

~

What is *tapas*? Panini tells us *tapas* is reflection, *ālochanā*. He is looking at the world, trying to find out what this world manifests, what is the Supreme Principle which guides this world, which accounts for the progress that this world has made from a molten mass of fire to the present reality when people like Swami Dayanand have been produced.

There is a great *rahasya* found there which accounts for the progress and order of the world. In other words, when we are called upon to practise *tapas*, we are called upon to practise our reason, our reflection, to look at the world, to try judge things by our capacity, to conform to the laws of reason and thought.

In that way he emphasized the rule of reason and pointed out that there is one Supreme God. He also gave freedom of conscience. People may look upon that Supreme as this or that or a third thing. That one Supreme Reality is made out by our heart, by our intelligence and by our will. It is made out in different ways, but we who quarrel about that do not know that the one Reality which is there is the One Supreme without a second.

If we really believe in God, if we believe that all human individuals are sparks or fragments of that divine fire, why is it that we have introduced hierarchical distinctions, distinctions of caste and outcaste, and imposed so many disabilities on our women? Here he has to say that if you believe in God, then you must be a believer in the equality of all men and women.

You cannot impose restrictions which forbid the study of the *Vedas* or the practice of the *Gāyatrī jāpa* to anyone in this world. By virtue of his manhood, of his humanity, everyone is a candidate for spiritual life. And nobody should be denied the privilege of pursuing the greatest fulfilment of his own nature.

So not only did he believe in the Supreme but he also enunciated a law of equality of men and women and urged that nobody should be prevented from having access to the spiritual wisdom and the spiritual rituals of our country.

~

He was a social reformer who had a crusading zeal, a powerful intellect and a fire in his heart when he looked at the social injustices. He tried to sweep them away with a drastic hand. This is also what the country requires today. That is why he went from place to place and told the people, 'If you are believers, all believers belong to the one family of God. If you believe in the Supreme, every human individual is a spark of the Supreme. Therefore, you must try to give the best opportunities for the fulfilment of each human individual.'

So, the worship of the One, and the services of man, irrespective of caste, colour and creed, are the two fundamental principles which he formulated. Not only did he formulate them, he went about preaching this gospel, and the Arya Samaj[1] has established many institutions which are today trying to perpetuate these things. Many of these have been incorporated in our social life and practice. Our social legislation after Independence gives equality to men and women; we have tried to remove the disabilities which subjected women to all sorts of atrocities. All these things have become today, a part of our social life.

We should not forget how much we owe to the inspiration of a great man like Swami Dayanand Saraswati; we are adopting the principles which he taught us.

We can strengthen our nation only if we are able to abolish all man-made distinctions, and if we coalesce into a homogeneous community and stand together as one nation. It is this which we are called upon to do now.

The teachings which Swami Dayanand Saraswati gave us are of great value today. They are of Supreme importance at a time when we are still bickering and fighting about all sorts of things. Intolerance has been the bane of India. Time and again this country has been subjected to all sorts of slavery. Why? On account of our internal divisions, on account of our mutual intolerance. If we do not learn from the past, we have to live the past over again. This is the lesson we have to instil into our minds.

If we are to learn from the past, the one lesson we need is: forget differences, do not quarrel with one another, believe in the One Supreme and look upon all people as children of that Supreme One.

References

1 Founded by Swami Dayanand Saraswati in 1875, it became the most powerful movement for Hindu social reform and revival of Vedic values in northern India.

Inaugurator of modern Indian renaissance.

FOUR

Raja Rammohan Roy

(Aug 14, 1774 – Sep 27, 1833)

Raja Rammohan Roy is described as the founder of modern India and the inaugurator of modern Indian renaissance. Renaissance is not merely revival. It takes up ancient wisdom and tries to reconcile it with modern enlightenment; and wherever there is a struggle between the two, it cuts out with a drastic hand whatever is repugnant to reason or to the moral sense.

Raja Rammohan Roy was a believer in human freedom, freedom in every sense of the term. He tried to emancipate the human mind from superstition, from obscurantism, for everything that lowers the dignity of man.

Tapas is reflection on the nature of the universe. Panini tells us, the first word is *lochnā*, the second is *ālochanā*, reflection on the nature of the universe. He winds up by saying that spirit is the Ultimate Reality; not matter or *ánnam*, not life or *prānā*, not mind or *manas*, not *vijñāna* or intelligence, but *ānanda* or spirit is the Ultimate Reality from which all the others emanate. India, which adopted the *Upaniṣads* as one of its sacred texts, deviated from their path and lost itself in ceremonial piety and scholastic disputations. It is the mark of a great genius to recall our minds to the fundamental truth.

Moreover, Rammohan Roy studied the classics of Hinduism, Islam and Christianity and found that pure theism was the substance of all religions. On the basis of such a kind of theism it will be possible to integrate not only communities in this country but the whole world. In one of the prayer songs given today, it is made out that there is one Supreme Lord, one Maker of this Universe, described differently. But by your heart, by your intelligence, by your will, you give that fact different descriptions, but the Ultimate Substance is one.

There are halting, imperfect descriptions of that One Supreme. If we are able to recognize the reality of the Supreme, we will not fall into controversial paths; because mystery is mystery and our attitude is one of silent adoration. Our words and minds are unable to comprehend the immense mystery of this universe. That is the attitude the human mind must adopt: the human mind is incapable of comprehending adequately the nature of that Supreme.

If we get back to this religion of truth, truth of universal love, then it will be possible for us to forget our petty differences, our trivialities on which we waste our lives; our bigotries and disputations will all lose their force and significance. A truly religious man, if he is authentically religious, will feel that every human being has the dignity, has the spark of Divine. Everyone is a fragment of that impersonal Brahmand, the Universe. You must help everyone to discard all things which prevent his inward life from manifesting itself.

When in this country people were downtrodden and our women were subjected to many disabilities, Raja Rammohan Roy raised his voice of protest and said that a country which called itself civilized must accept the basic principle of equality, the equality of all human beings; so long as some people were treated as inferior and others as superior, you were not truly civilized men. This concept of equality was there in our religion in its pristine state. In ancient times women were entitled to every kind of privilege that men had: privileges were given equally to men and women. But centuries passed and this whole concept of equality was dropped and we suffered as a result.

If this country passed through degradation and subjection, it was because we were disloyal to the ideals that we professed. We proclaim high cause of the suffering and subjection to which this country has been put. And if we are to get rid of all these things, we must abolish the disabilities. In practice complete equality should be given to men and women, to the fallen and downtrodden as well as to the privileged.

Raja Rammohan Roy said that he was also for freedom from political subjection, from political tyranny. His contributions to Bengali prose, to the freedom of the Indian press and to love of humanity, and the way in which he appealed to the French Minister and the British legislators about freedom for India, are well known.

There is no question that the great ideals for which Raja Rammohan Roy stood — religion of truth, social equality, unity of mankind — are still our distant goals. We have not realized them. So the message which Raja Rammohan Roy gave us, a message which still has validity, as the ideals for which he lived and died are yet unrealized. They have to be implemented by everyone of us. He was, of course, subjected to persecution, to suffering. That is the lot of all great men. Let me assure you that the world is shaped by the genuine souls who contradict the world most: it is these people who convert the world.

Raja Rammohan Roy stood for equality against caste, for science against superstition, for democracy against dictatorship, for the religion of truth and not a religion of superstition.

A harmonious blend of science,
art and religion.

FIVE

Acharya Jagdis Bose
(Nov 30, 1858 – Nov 23, 1937)

I had the privilege of knowing Jagdis Bose for a number of years when I was a member of the Calcutta University staff. He was the first Indian member of the International Committee of Intellectual Co-operation. Anyone who came to know him was impressed not only by his scientific imagination and inventive skill but also by his pride and patriotism. In him was a harmonious blend of science, art and religion.

The Institute[1] which he founded is an illustration of his integrated outlook. It is not merely a laboratory but a temple. The working table is an altar. The speech which he made on the occasion of the dedication of the Institute to the nation is remarkable; it thrills you with emotions of our past glory and inspires us to greater achievements in the future. Despite all obstacles, but with a firm conviction that truth would prevail, he carried on his impassioned inquiry and research, surmounted the doubt of the learned and the scepticism of the cynics, and established his eminence as a pioneer in the border regions of physics and physiology.

His life and work are a triumph of character over circumstances.

India has had a long and continuous history in the development of science. In the seventh chapter of *Chhāndogya Upaniṣad* are mentioned the different kinds of knowledge which the learned Nārada says that he knows:

> *ṛg-vedam, yajur-vedam, sama-vedam, atharvanam, ithihasa-puranam, vedanam vedam, pitrayam, rasim, daivam, nidhim, vakovakyam, ekayunam, deva-vidyam, brahma-vidyam, bhuta-vidyam, ksatra-vidyam, naksatra-vidyam, sarpadevajana-vidyam.*

The *Ṛg-Veda*, the *Yajur-Veda*, the *Sāma-Veda*, the *Athārvāṇam*, the epics and the *Purāṇas*, grammar which is the *Veda* of the *Vedas*, propitiation of the Fathers, the science of the numbers, the science of portents, the science of time, logic, ethics and politics, the science of the gods, the science of sacred knowledge, the science of elemental spirits, the science of serpents and the fine arts.

Indians were greatly interested in ascertaining the laws which govern the different aspects of the universe. They made profound contributions to mathematics, astronomy, grammar, logic, natural sciences and medicine. But unfortunately, for some centuries, the scientific genius of India lay dormant.

In the nineteenth century there was a revival and India again entered into the stream of world science. Dr. Mahendralal Sircar (1833-1904) emphasized the importance of scientific knowledge for India's progress. With his passion for science and thirst for knowledge, he founded the Indian Association for the Cultivation of Science (IACS), providing facilities for research in all branches of science. Many eminent people, including Professors C.V. Raman and K.S. Krishnan worked in this Association.

~

Jagdis Bose was a pioneer in research in natural sciences. The great plant physiologist Professor Heberlandt of Germany after a lecture-demonstration by Jagdis Bose observed: 'It is not an accident that it should have been an Indian investigator who has in such a high measure perfected the methods of the physiology of irritability. In Professor Bose there lives and moves that ancient Indian spirit which he has carried to its utmost limits — metaphysical speculation and introspection, wholly withdrawn from the world of sense... this same spirit has been brought to light by its modern representative, who is our guest today, with such an extraordinarily developed faculty for observation and such an ecstasy in scientific experimentation.'

Some of the profound insights of the Indian seers which received scientific verification in the researches of Jagdis Bose.

1. The Indian seers look upon the world as a whole and not an aggregate. It is *Puranam*, in the words of the *Upaniṣad*. It is a universe not a multiverse. Just as in the microcosm of the human system we have *ānna, prānā, manas, vijñāna* and *ānanda*, so also we have them in the macrocosm of the cosmos. *Piṇḍa* and *brahmāṇḍa* reflect each other.

2. The world is not a dead expanse but a living universe. The world is called *jagat*, that which moves or is alive. The throb of life is to be found everywhere. The *Īśa Upaniṣad* asks us to know that all this, whatever moves in this moving world is steeped in God — *isavasyam idam sarvam yat kim ca jagatyam jagat.*
3. Nature makes no leaps. There is continuity between the inorganic and the organic, between the living and the animal consciousness. Dharmottara[2] in his *Nyāyā-bindu-tikā* notices the contraction of leaves in the night — *svaah ratrau patra-samkocah.*

   Udayanacarya mentions phenomena in plants as in the human body: of life, death, sleep, waking, disease, taking medicines, etc.[3]

Jaina and Vaisesika writers, Gunaratna and Samkara-misra mention these characteristics of plants. The sensitiveness to touch of plants like the *mimosa pudica* (*lajjavati lata*) is noticed. Plants are said to have latent consciousness and are susceptible to pleasure and pain, *antaḥsaṃjnă bhavanty ete sukha-duḥkha-samanvitāḥ*. Udyana speaks of the plants as having a dull unmanifested consciousness — *atimandantahsam jnitaya.* Sanskrit poets speak of the *suryamukhi* flowers, which open out in sunlight and shut in its absence. The intuitions of our seers were given empirical verification by Jagdis Bose.

Life activities in the animal and the plant were generally treated as dissimilar. Animals respond to a shock by movement while plants maintain an attitude of passivity even under a succession of blows. Jagdis Bose writes:

> 'Animal tissues give electric signs of irritation; ordinary plants, according to leading electro-physiologists, show no such signs of excitement. In the animal, again, there

His life and

work are a triumph of character

over circumstances.

> is an evolution of wonderful nervous system... In the vegetal organism on the other hand, all authorities are unanimous in declaring that there is no such thing as a nervous impulse... The two streams of life were said to flow side by side, governed by laws which were altogether different.'

Jagdis Bose held a different view. He said that the nervous impulse in the plant and the animal was similar. He tried to demonstrate these views by means of delicately contrived instruments.

The transition from matter to life, from life to mind may be represented by a slope rather than a staircase. Throughout the cosmos we have continuity and bonds which unite. Jagdis Bose was interested in the latter. While we emphasize the continuity, we should not overlook the creative advance.

A small pebble and a mango seed may be like each other in size, colour, weight, but the difference between them is significant. The pebble may remain the same for a hundred years but the seed has in it the power to become something else. If the conditions are favourable it will gather materials from the soil, from the rain and moisture in the air, from the light and heat of the sun. In time it may become a large tree which may produce in its turn fruits and seeds with the same capacity. The form which the pebble holds is more rigid than the subtle essence realized in the tree. The tree, unlike the pebble, while persevering towards its end, passes through a cyclic pattern unknown to the pebble. It grows, matures, ages and dies. Unlike the pebble it is subject to disease and is able to reproduce itself.

Science has done many wonderful things but it has not yet explained, much less produced, organic growth and reproduction. The chemical, electrical and electronic process cannot do what a single grain of wheat does, germinate in the spring time. While there is continuity between matter and life there is also a deep difference.

Between life and mind there is continuity. Is the mind always present wherever there is life, say in the organic cell? Is there a boundary between living organism to which mental qualities can be attributed and those to which they cannot?

In his address on the day when he gave his Research Institute to the nation, Jagdis Bose said:

> In the pursuit of my investigations I was unconsciously led into the border region of physics and physiology and was amazed to find boundary lines vanishing.

Inorganic matter was found anything but inert; it also was a thrill under the action of multitudinous forces that play on it. A universal reaction seemed to bring together metal, plant and animal under a common law. They all exhibited essentially the same phenomena of fatigue and depression together with possibilities of recovery and of exaltation yet, also that of permanent irresponsiveness which is associated with death. These results were demonstrated by experiments to show the response of matter and the revelations of plant life foreshadowing the wonders of animal life.

Similarly, there is continuity between plant and animal life but life and mind are also different. Impulses from the outer world are transmitted to the brain and constitute its sense data. These are the raw material for perception. We know that consciousness is affected by chemical substances, alcohol, opium, mescaline, anaesthetics and also by concussion. We do not understand what happens in the conscious mind when we have perception, reflection, choice, decision, violation.

Sir Charles Sherrington in his *Man on his Nature* writes: 'The search in that (energy) scheme for a scale of equivalence between energy and mental experience arrives at none. The two, for all I can do, remain refractorily apart. They seem to me disparate; not mutually convertible, untranslatable from one into the other.' In his *Rede Lecture* at Cambridge, he said: 'Strictly we have to regard the relation of mind to brain as still not merely unsolved but still devoid of a basis for its very beginning.' In his last utterance on this subject in a broadcast symposium on 'The Physical Basis of the Mind', his final words were: 'Aristotle, two thousand years ago, was asking how is the mind attached to the body. We are asking that question still.'

True science humbles its votary. It makes him realize how little he knows and how vast is the unknown. No wonder Jagdis Bose, as a seeker for knowledge, felt the mystery underlying the universe. The process of evolution, the stream of creative activity which rolls on, never resting, this perpetual procession of events which we call *saṃsāra* is not self-sufficient or self-maintaining. Look at the succession, a molten mass of fire. The emergence of life, creatures whose forehead recedes, whose teeth protrude, with grunts and groans trying by painful steps to walk on earth, others with articulate speech covered with a sheepskin, carrying a sharp stone and an axe.

Man rubs two sticks together and spark flies, the flame dances. A group of shepherds driving a herd of cattle before them, stop at the edge of a river, glance at the stars and lift their hands in mute appeal for safety and solace. From a nebula, a cloud of gas drifting about in space, the human race has slowly emerged into a Valmiki or a Kālidāsa, a Shakespeare or a Goethe, a Newton or an Einstein or Tagore or a Bose. Could it have happened without the inspiration of a higher power working through and directing the process? The *Upaniṣads* speak of this world as the manifestation of Brahman. Charles Darwin wrote in his *The Descent of Man*: 'That grand sequence of events which our minds refuse to accept as result of blind chance. The understanding revolts at such a conclusion.'

The simple and deep-seated conviction in the human mind that there is a unitary whole which manifests as a manifold, is for the scientist a hypothesis which calls for experimental testimony. For the religious seer it is an act of faith that proves itself in experience. There is no opposition between science and superstition.

Throughout this cosmic process we have continuity and progress. We cannot revive the past but we can build better on the foundations furnished by it. The present shall grow into a nobler future through our efforts. The living spirit of the scientist is a reflection of the Divine mystery. *Tát tvam ási*. Man is made in the image of God and so has to participate in creation. It was Bose's ambition that our people should carry on investigation and research, enrich the world by their results and reach the goal of an enduring brotherhood. Let us work for this goal for the good of mankind and the glory of God.

Jagaddhitāya Kṛṣṇāya.

References

1 Bose Institute or Bose Bigyan Mandir, is a premier research institute in India and also the oldest. It was established in 1917 by Jagdis Bose widely acknowledged as father of modern scientific research in India.

2 8th century Buddhist author of important works on Pramana (valid cognition). His only Sanskrit work now available is Ny*ā*y*ā* bindutika.

3 *vrksadayah prati-niyata-bhoktrydhisthitah jivana-maronasvapna-jagarana-roga-bhesaja-prayoga...* (See B.N.Seal: *The Positive Sciences of the Ancient Hindus* (1915), pp. 173-176).

Living without fear or favour.

SIX

Gopal Krishna Gokhale

(May 9, 1866 – Feb 19, 1915)

The attempt of Gokhale was to spiritualize politics. Politics in those days was not so very complicated as it happens to be today, yet even those days he felt the need for spiritualization of politics.

Today when we have power, when we have authority, when it is possible for us to do so much, it is more necessary than ever to spiritualize politics. Politics mostly is a region full of ego, pride, prejudice, self-interest, love of power. These are so much to the top of our mind that most of us go about saying, 'There is hoarding, there is corruption, there is dishonesty.' These are the complaints which are heard most often. It is not for me to say if these are justified are not. All that I say is that the spirit of honesty, integrity and dedication are necessary principles in undertaking public work.

Are we or are we not *therefore* to follow his example? If we look at the way in which our Assemblies and Parliament are functioning these days, we realise that there is an urgent need for spiritualization of politics; every person who enters the Assembly or Parliament should regard himself as a servant of humanity, as a servant of the people of India and should refrain from doing anything which is likely to impair the prestige or respect for the State.

These days in selecting candidates for legislatures or other public bodies we do not seem to insist on the purity of the means. Instead we seem to be possessed by considerations of caste or community and not those of character or capacity. The disorder in the country is very much traceable to this factor also.

Public work, Gokhale felt, should have intellectual and moral foundations. Leadership, to be effective, should have moral authority. His attempt was to spiritualize politics. Anyone who leads a dedicated life, who is devoted to truth, and who avoids intrigue and factionalism in public life, he is a religious man though he may call himself a pagan or agnostic.

~

In our country, once upon a time, the question was: 'What constitutes the principle of good life? Who is supposed to be a good Man?'

The ancient *Upaniṣad says*: 'Didn't you hear the thunder clap? What did it say? *da da da: datta, damyata, dayadhavam* — charity, self-control, compassion — these are the principles which constitute a good life. It is these principles which we have to imbibe and adopt in our life, if the level of our political and public life has to go up. Gokhale gave us an example of that in whatever work he undertook, inwhatever speeches he made.

In our student days we used to read about his speeches in the newspapers. We were all struck by his intense patriotism, when he rebutted the charge that universities were seats of sedition and that educational institutions were breeding people in a kind of inflammatory atmosphere.

When we heard all those things we were greatly thrilled. But what constitutes his greatness?

His greatness consisted in making a thorough preparation of any subject that he took up, a careful study of facts followed by an objective and scrupulous fact-based judgement and justified condemnation or approval.

Those who undertake public life today will have to regard themselves as whole time workers, make a thorough study of the political problems of the country and then come to judgements which are reasoned and reasonable. That is what they should do. But are they doing it?

~

From Gokhale we inherited a tradition — a tradition which calls upon us not to sacrifice the individual at the altar of the State or any kind of State system but to protect the individual, protect his rights, regard individual as sacred. That gives us the justification for the attitude which we are adopting.

It is necessary, therefore, that we should regard the individual as the end and not the State as the end. We should regard individual rights as inviolable. It may be necessary to sacrifice our life, but we should do so with all respect to ourselves and with integrity.

'It is my ambition to become Muslim Gokhale.'

Mohd. Ali Jinnah

In spite of all the objectives which we have professed, there are social disparities in our society, disparities of high and low, of rich and poor, of high castes and outcastes, untouchables, etc. Have we even come to somewhere near the end of the task? Is not our present state of affairs a challenge? Are we not called upon to adopt the right kind of attitude in handling these problems?

Why did Gandhi feel attracted to Gokhale? For the simple reason that Gokhale would not surrender or sacrifice truth for the sake of any political idea or ideology. His attitude was to stand firm and give his opinion without fear or favour, without any ill-will or malice toward anybody. He commanded the respect even of his opponents. Whether they liked him or not, whether they liked his opinions or not, they had high regard for his integrity and for the careful and honest study he made of the facts on any subject or topic that he discussed or spoke about.

He will be remembered for long years for the brilliant Budget speeches he made in the Central Assembly.

In accordance with the traditions of our country Gokhale emphasized the need for renunciation in public life. *Servaṁ vastu bhayānvitam bhuvi nṛṇām vairāgyaṁ evābhavam*. While everything in this world is fraught with fear for men, renunciation alone gives fearlessness.

When the comforts of the world were in Gokhale's reach and could have been his, he left them and devoted his rich talents to the service of the country. Renunciation is the principle of a good life. Men are great not by what they acquire but by what they renounce. Those who engage in public work should not look upon it as a career with glittering prizes.

At the age of twenty years Gokhale joined the Deccan Education Society and served it for twenty years on a small allowance of Rs. 75 per month. In 1905 he founded the Servants of India Society[1] and set up a body of dedicated persons. The members participated in varied activities — education, journalism, politics, tribal welfare, etc. all guided by Gokhale's dictum:

> 'Public life must be spiritualized. Love of country must so fill the heart that all else shall appear of little importance by its side. A fervent patriotism which rejoices at every opportunity of sacrifice for the Motherland, a dauntless heart which refuses to be turned back from its object by difficulty or danger, a deep faith in the purpose of Providence which nothing can shake — equipped with these, the worker must start on his mission and reverently seek the joy of spending himself in the service of the country.'

No wonder that Gandhi claimed Gokhale as his political guru. His meetings with him left a lasting influence on Gandhi and he heeded his advice to tour the length and breadth of the country, 'with eyes and ears open, but mouth shut', absorbing, learning, digesting, but not reacting. Although Gandhi later adopted civil disobedience, which was somewhat contrary to Gokhale's core thinking, his debt to Gokhale was immeasurable.

Gokhale insisted not only on intellectual efficiency but also moral responsibility for the members of the Society. In the Society he enrolled members like G.K. Deodhar, a valiant fighter for social reforms; N.M. Joshi, who influenced the Trade Union Movement; Srinivasa Sastri, who served in varied capacities; he had with as the first member H.N. Kunzru, a man of integrity and uprightness. Gandhi and Nehru seriously thought of joining the Society.

When Gokhale visited South Africa in 1912, a well-known statesman-senator said to him, 'Sir, when men like you visit our country, they purify the atmosphere.'

~

Life is one whole. Political progress and social reform cannot be separated. Life cannot be compartmentalized. Gokhale sympathized with the poor and the oppressed. In his evidence before the Welby[2] Commission he gave expression to the growing poverty of the country under British rule.

Gokhale had deep faith in democratic principles — in civil liberties, in free press, in free association without hatred of racial discrimination of any type, in decent standards of living for all. He was an ardent advocate of free and compulsory education.

Political or religious reformers who are liberal are rarely critical of the conditions around them and do not have the feeling of hate. They are free from all negative feelings and instead their focus is on improving the existent conditions.

Gokhale's liberalism did not forbid him from adopting Gandhi's passive resistance. In a speech on Indians in Transvaal at a public meeting in Bombay in 1909, Gokhale said:

> 'Passive Resistance to an unjust law or an apprehensive measure is a refusal to acquiesce to that law or measure and a readiness to suffer the penalty instead, which may be prescribed as an alternative. If we strongly and clearly and conscientiously feel the grave injustice of a law, and

'The greatest saint and soldier of our national righteousness whose life was a sacrament and whose death was a sacrifice in the cause of Indian unity.'

Sarojini Naidu

there is no other way to obtain redress, I think refusal to acquiesce, taking the consequence of such refusal, is the only course left to those who place conscience and self-respect above their material or immediate interests.'

The problems facing India in Gokhale's time were formidable. Though he served all aspects of our life in a brilliant and wholehearted manner he was conscious of the long distance we have to traverse before we reach the goal. He had faith in the destiny of his country:

> '...it will, no doubt, be given to our countrymen of the future generations, to serve India by their successes; we of the present generation must be content to serve her by our failures. For hard though it be, out of those failures, the strength will come, which in the end will accomplish great tasks.'

Sarojini Naidu described Gokhale as 'the greatest saint and soldier of our national righteousness whose life was a sacrament and whose death was a sacrifice in the cause of Indian unity.'

Ministers of good things are like torches, a light to others and destruction to themselves.

~

The lesson which we have to learn from Gokhale's life is that if we are to improve ourselves, we need to have an element of reverence for Mahadev Govind Ranade, for Dadabhai Naoroji, for Pherozeshah Mehta, and for Gandhi. That element of reverence is fast disappearing from our life.

It is this that we should re-emphasize. We should be grateful to people who put us on the right track.

And next to reverence was his principle of renunciation. Things come and go. Prestige disappears in a few days. A great man of today is a fallen hero of tomorrow. That is how it is, *Vibhavo Śaiva Śaśvataḥ*. All this pomp and glory are not eternal.

Reverence for life and renunciation, if we adopt these two principles we will serve Gokhale and his memory well.

~

Our country has been famous for its great sages and saints. History is not a battle of kings, nor is it merely an account of what happened between dynasties. History is a march of social changes, of new economic structures, of new movements which happen in this world. They are the things which matter in the life-time of a nation. So far as our nation is concerned, the things that happened in Gokhale's time, the work that was done, the political movements, social movements, religious reforms, all these things which happened, stand together. They are not to be kept apart. They are all parts of one whole.

It is essential, so far as our country is concerned, that we should stick to the framework of our religions, our widest landmarks, so to say, which will always be there, because the scientists may touch the periphery but nobody touches the centre.

If we concentrate on the centre of our being, we will realize that there is an aspect, a universal nature, a universal right, which gives utterance to all the other things we have. In other words, our intellect, our mind, our growth, all these things are the expressions of that universal centre which each one has. Because we are trying to forget that centre, many of us are getting alienated from ourselves and are suffering from neuroses and disturbances.

Let us develop reverence, let us develop respect, for the central principle of our being and let us have renunciation. We will go forward.

What touches human hearts is the power of faith. It comes only to those who have suffered greatly. Though Gokhale knew Dadabhai Naoroji, Gandhi and Tilak, his heart was given to Mahadev Ranade[3], who gave him the ideals which Gokhale illustrated in his life. In the prospectus of the Deccan Sabha, Ranade said:

> Liberalism and moderation will be the watch-words of our Association. The spirit of liberalism implies freedom from race and creed prejudices and, a steady devotion to all that seeks to do justice between man and man, giving to the rulers the loyalty that is due to the law that they are bound to administer, but securing at the same time to the people the equality which is their right under the law. Moderation implies the conditions of never vainly aspiring after the impossible or after remote ideals but striving each day to take the next step in the order of natural growth by doing the work that lies nearest to our hands in a spirit of compromise and fairness.

Gokhale easily identified himself with the condition of his people and consistently tried to raise it.

Whatever work Gokhale undertook, he threw himself into it, heart and soul. As a Professor (later Principal) of English and Mathematics in Fergusson College or as a member of the Central Legislative Council, or as a member of the Bombay University or the Poona Municipality, thoroughness marked his work. Gandhi came to know Gokhale well and felt that he was the one whom he could accept as his guru. Gandhi said of Gokhale:

> He seemed to me, all I wanted as a political worker — pure as a crystal, gentle as a lamb, brave as a lion, and chivalrous to a fault. It does not matter to me that he may not have been any of these things. It was enough for me that I could discover no fault in him to cavil at. He was, and remains for me, the most perfect man in the political field.

References

[1] Servants of India Society founded by Gopal Krishna Gokhale in 1905 was the first secular organization in the country to be devoted to the underprivileged, rural and tribal people, emergency relief work, literacy, and other social causes.

[2] Welby Commission — In 1895, the Royal Commission on the Administration of Expenditure of India, known as the Welby Commission, was set up to look into Indian expenditures and improve the economic condition India by reducing excessive expenses. Among those who provided of excessive or unjust payments by the then Government was Gokhale.

[3] Mahadev Govind Ranade was a judge, scholar and social reformer and Gokhale regarded him as his philosopher and guide. He worked with him in the Sarvajanik Sabha, and edited its quarterly journal that addressed public questions of the day in a frank and fearless manner.

Unafraid and forthright, one who laid the foundation of Indian nationalism.

SEVEN

Bal Gangadhar Tilak

(July 23, 1856 – Aug 1, 1920)

When I was a student in the early years of the twentieth century, for the youth of India, the name of Tilak meant burning patriotism, rare courage, indomitable will and dedication to the freedom of India.

In the second decade, I happened to write an article in July 1911, on *The Ethics of the Bhagavadgītā and Kant* which attracted the attention of Tilak who was then in Mandalay prison, Burma (now Myanmar). Late Shri N.C. Kelkar had requested me for the article which he had then sent to Tilak. In due course the article was returned to me with Tilak's marginal notes. Later, to my great joy, I found that Tilak had mentioned my name as one who supported an activistic interpretation of the *Bhagavadgītā* in the preface of his monumental work, *Gita Rahasya.*[1]

Even the liberated are called upon to work for world solidarity, *loka-saṃgraha;* for the good of the world, the glory of God, *Jagad-hitāya-kṛṣṇaya. Gītā* is a *yogasastra.* Yoga is *karmasu kauśalam*, skill in action. *Samatvaṁ yoga ucyate,* equanimity is yoga. *Kṛṣṇa* is yogesvara. He is the Lord of action.

vivekī sarvadā muktaḥ kurvato nasti kartrta
alepa-vadam asritya sri-kṛṣṇa janakau yatha.

The spiritual and social sides go together.

Tilak's life was a demonstration of this great ideal of Karma Yoga. The saints of Maharashtra — Jnaneshwar, Eknath, Tukaram, Ramdas — proclaim that disinterested service of man is the worship of God.

In ordinary circumstances Tilak would have lived a scholar's life, and made outstanding contributions to Oriental Studies and Mathematics. For a brief period he taught mathematics at Fergusson College[2], Poona (now Pune) but as a member of a subject nation he believed he had no alternative except to take part in politics. In 1890, he left teaching for open political working and began a mass movement towards independence by emphasising religious and cultural revival.

> Once when asked: 'What portfolio will you take up when we obtain Swaraj? Will you be Prime Minister or Foreign Minister?' His answer showed where his heart lay.
>
> 'Under Swaraj, I will become a Professor of Mathematics and retire from political life. I detest politics. I still wish to write a book on Differential Calculus. The country is in a very bad way and so I am compelled to take part in politics.'

Tilak had a long political career agitating for Indian autonomy from the British rule. Before Gandhi, he was the most widely known Indian political leader. Unlike his fellow Maharashtrian contemporary, Gokhale, Tilak was considered a radical Nationalist but a Social conservative. He was imprisoned on a number of occasions that included a long stint at Mandalay jail. At one stage in his political life he was called 'the father of Indian unrest' by British author, journalist and diplomat, Sir Valentine Chirol.

He was not in sympathy with the methods of those who were then called Moderates[3]. He transformed the political movement limited to the upper classes into a national one. By the use of popular festivals and through the medium of his well-known Marathi paper *Kesari*[4] he spread the message of 'Swaraj as our birth right' to the common people.

He advocated a vigorous programme of national education, Swadeshi, boycott of all things foreign, passive resistance, including non-payment of taxes. His plan included prohibition and removal of untouchability.

In his hands the political movement became a revolutionary one, but revolution is not to be confused with barricades and bloodshed. He repudiated methods of violence. When political and social conflicts were tense, he affirmed that in such matters 'fanaticism is suicidal'[5].

In 1904 when violence was in the air, Tilak wrote in *Kesari*: 'The British administration does not depend upon any one person at any time. Therefore, nobody can get Swaraj by killing an officer and even if one could get it, murder is absolutely

'Swaraj is the foundation and not the height of our future prosperity. We have to build a new nation, develop a new character, live the principles which we advocate, faith in spiritual values, love of country and tolerance for views from which we differ.'

Bal Gangadhar Tilak

reprehensible. It is cowardice to incite anyone to commit murder. But if necessary, we should suffer for our convictions.'

When he was condemned to a six-year sentence (1908-14)[6] to be served in Mandalay jail, Judge Dinshaw D. Davar asked him if he had anything to say, Tilak said:

> 'All that I wish to say is that, in spite of the verdict of the jury, I still maintain that I am innocent. There are higher powers that rule the destinies of men and nations; and I think, it may be the will of Providence that the cause I represent may be benefited more by my suffering than by my pen and tongue and remaining free.'

No wonder, when condemned to a similar sentence to Mandalay in 1922[7], Gandhi had replied to the judge: 'I would say one word. Since you have done me the honour of recalling the trial of the late Lokamanya Bal Gangadhar Tilak, I just want to say that I consider it to be the proudest privilege and honour to be associated with his name...'

While sentencing Gandhi, the judge had observed, 'You, Mr Gandhi, will not consider it unreasonable, I think, that you should be classed with Mr. Tilak.'

~

Tilak repeatedly said: 'Swaraj is the foundation and not the height of our future prosperity. We have to build a new nation, develop a new character, live the principles which we advocate, faith in spiritual values, love of country and tolerance for views from which we differ.'

The perspective of history will record that in Tilak we had an Indian, true and great, proud of his country's past and confident about its future, a patriot unafraid and forthright, one who laid the foundations of Indian nationalism and revolutionary struggle through non-violent political action.

References

1 *Gita Rahasya* or *Shrimad Bhagwadgita Rahasya* is a 2-part book in Marathi written by Tilak while imprisoned in Madalay jail. The 1st part is philosophical exposition and the 2nd part is translation and commentary of Gītā.

2 Fergusson College was founded in 1885 by Deccan Education Society, which amongst others had Tilak as one of its founding members.

3 Tilak opposed the moderate views of Gopal Krishna Gokhale, and supported nationalists Bipin Chandra Pal and Lala Lajpat Rai. The triumvirate was referred to as 'Lal-Bal-Pal'. At the 1907 annual session of the Congress Party in Surat there was sharp difference of opinion over the selection of the new president and the party split into the nationalist faction led by Lal, Bal, Pal supported by other nationalists like Aurobindo Ghose, and V.O. Chidambaram Pillai.

4 Marathi newspaper founded by Balgangadhar Tilak.

5 *Kesari*, 7.6.1892.

6 In 1909 Tilak was tried in the court of Judge Davar and a special jury, for sedition in respect of certain articles published in the *Kesari* in May and June 1908.

7 Gandhi was also tried for sedition for publishing articles in *Young India* in September and December 1921 and in February 1922.

Faith in the spirit of man to mould history.

EIGHT

Motilal Nehru

(Aug 22, 1861 – Feb 6, 1931)

The services which Shri Motilal Nehru rendered to this country's struggle, progress and prosperity are many, varied and outstanding. But I am concerned with the special contribution which he made to the development of parliamentary institutions. He was the Chairman of All-Parties[1] Committee which was asked to draft a Constitution for our country in 1928. Despite many kindles, he Committee completed ... its Report commonly called Nehru Report and presents it in the fourth session of the All Parties Committee in August, 1928. It was the first attempt at drawing up a constitution of free India. The draft Constitution; included, among its features, the declaration of rights and the setting up of a judiciary with a Supreme Court at its apex. Parliamentary democracy was the primary purpose.

He not only taught us about Parliamentary democracy, but he knew that no freedom was worth its name unless it brought about national cohesion. He was aware of the way in which religion was confused with bigotry, a kind of superiority complex that one had the monopoly of all truth and that others were groping in the dark; he was aware that it was one's duty to get rid of that feeling. He knew the dangers of such kind of attitude. He protested against the mixing of religion with politics and insisted that all our brethren must be considered as citizens of our country and that they should not be looked down upon on the basis of caste. He asked us to build up a coherent society.

The purposes of our Constitution or society are based on the principles which he framed.

The purposes are there but we have to achieve them by our own drive, energy, enterprise, organization and by the stigma of the love of power and the love of self-interest, and by development of rectitude. These are essential for the carrying out of the aims which we have set for ourselves.

There is another thing which I should like to remind about: he served on the Skeen Committee[2], a committee which was entrusted with the setting up of National Defence Colleges.

We are all working for a time when armies, etc. would not be necessary. But that time is still far away. But until that time comes, it is essential for us to keep our armies intact, to see that they are modern and well-equipped, so that no people can take liberties with us. It is therefore incumbent on us to remember what he did on the Skeen Committee.

Apart from his parliamentary work, Motilal Nehru laid the greatest stress on communal harmony and unity. It was not a mere tactical move on his part, but a deep-felt conviction, a part of his very being.

When the country was torn by communal strife and when bitterness and violence were rampant, Gandhi undertook a fast. Motilal presided over the Unity Conference and on September 26, 1924, the Conference resolved that 'the utmost freedom of conscience and religion was essential, and condemned any desecration of places of worship, to whatever faith they may belong, and any persecution or punishment of any person for adopting or reverting to any faith; and it further condemned any attempts by compulsion to convert people to one's faith or to secure or enforce one's own religious observance at the cost of the rights of others.'

This faith in communal harmony and religious fellowship is needed even today. Though we suffered in the past for our religious bigotry and communal dissensions, we have not yet learnt the needed lesson. The canker of communalism is deep-seated in our body politics. We should do our utmost to root it out and cleanse our natures.

Motilal was a radical reformer not out of any false sentiment but for a very good reason. Communal passions are inconsistent with the true spirit of religion or the traditions of our country.

~

Faith in the infallibility of any individual or nation is at the root of all conflicts in this world. It breeds fanaticism, sets up dictatorships, brings about fascism of the mind which has often drenched this earth with blood and tears. It is, therefore, essential for us to avoid that kind of dogmatic attitude.

A democratic attitude requires appreciation that the other man may possibly be right and that we ourselves may be in the wrong, an attitude of modesty, humility, good manners and charity — these are the essential qualities of a democratic frame of mind. If we wish to work democratic institutions successfully and satisfactorily then opinionatedness; dogmatism, an idea that we alone have the monopoly of truth and that others are revelling in the dark, are things which we should avoid.

In international relations, this requires us to settle all outstanding differences by persuasion, negotiation and mediation. A climate of international sobriety has to be engendered if the world is to be made a happy home for the different nations of the world. In both these respects, Shri Motilal Nehru set us a great example.

He was Leader of the Opposition in the Central Legislative Assembly for six years. The Opposition had a number of members belonging to different persuasions. He brought them all together, organized them into a single team and made the then Assembly reject four successive budgets. He moved a Resolution on self-government for India which was passed by 76 votes to 48, the opponents being official and other nominees.

The great point about his achievement was that he had no malice in his heart, no bitterness, and that he commanded the confidence and affection of his followers and the respect and admiration of his opponents. The whole thing took place in a quiet and dignified way.

There was no greater problem in our country then than the achievement of self-government. In the Central Assembly was waged a battle between Indian nationalism and foreign domination and he prepared the ground for the achievement of freedom.

He gave us a magnificent example of dignified, disciplined behaviour which we should remember whenever we enter the precincts of Parliament.

~

In his political activities, two things stand out prominently. He was a great organizer, a great parliamentarian, and as the leader of the Swaraj Party in the Central Assembly, he set standards which we are striving to follow. From the visitors' gallery, I saw him on occasions at work in the Central Assembly as the Leader of the Opposition. Most distinguished in appearance, he led the Opposition with great astuteness, legal acumen and parliamentary skill.

I met Motilal Nehru for the first time when he came to Calcutta for presiding over the Congress session in 1928. In the same year he produced what is called the Nehru Report, our first effort at Constitution-making. I saw him also when he was leading the Swaraj Party[3] in the Central Assembly.

I met him again a few weeks before his death when he was undergoing treatment in Calcutta. His thoughts in those last days were about Swaraj for which he worked with such devotion and fervour. On his death-bed at Allahabad, Motilal Nehru was waiting for Gandhi. On his arrival Gandhi said to Motilal Nehru, 'We shall surely win Swaraj, if you survive this crisis.' Motilal Nehru replied, 'I am going soon, Mahatmaji, and I shall not be here to see Swaraj. But I know you have won it and will soon have it.'

Jawaharlal Nehru told Gandhi that in the last moments of his life, Motilal repeated the *Gāyatrī Mantra* though he had never uttered it for nearly 40 years. Says the mantra, God is no longer an irate father or a stern judge but the Light of Lights, *Jyotisam Jyotih*, Spirit of Light shining in the future, a Light towards which we all endeavour to advance with the faltering steps owing to our own unworthiness.

Our greatest sorrow is that he did not live to see that day.

~

It is possible to give a long list of the attributes and achievements of late Pandit Motilal Nehru, his qualities of leadership and warm humanity, his patience and persistence, his determination and energy, his courage and force. All these have stamped his mark indelibly on the public life of our country. However, I shall confine myself to the political and social activities of Motilal Nehru.

The credit for Motilal's entry into politics goes to Gandhi, apart from the forces of history. 'He is no brave man whose spirit does not rise when things are at their worst.'

Though accustomed to a very comfortable life and regarded as a great admirer of Western style and manners, he subjected himself to the discipline which Gandhi imposed on his followers. Gandhi made spinning the basis of his constructive programme. Spinning and wearing of *khaddar* had become obligatory for political workers; *khaddar* became the bond of sympathy between the political workers and the millions of Indians. He cast aside his foreign dress and put on *khaddar* in Indian style and looked even more impressive and attractive in his new style.

He organized opposition to the Simon Commission in 1928[4]. He joined the Civil Disobedience Movement in 1930[5] and suffered imprisonment.

He presided over the All-Parties Conference and drew up a Constitution for the country. The same year, 1928, he was the President of the Calcutta session of the Indian National Congress. It was a great joy for him to see Jawaharlal take over from him as Congress President. He quoted a Persian couplet which said, 'What the father has not been able to achieve, the son will.' He said that it would be 'the head of Gandhiji and the voice of Jawaharlal.'

In December 1929, the Lahore Congress Session under the Presidentship of Jawaharlal Nehru passed a resolution about the independence of India. It was passed by an overwhelming majority exactly at midnight and with it the New Year and the new era commenced.

The name of Motilal Nehru will be permanently inscribed in the annals of our history not only for his individual contribution, but for his greatest and noblest gift to this nation and the world, Jawaharlal Nehru. Motilal's whole family was inspired by his example and with the influence of Gandhi, became a part of the national movement.

He had an enfranchised mind, free from all prejudices, hospitable to all good influences, Hindu, Muslim and British.

Deep down he had faith in Indian culture and its freedom of spirit, its capacity for healing the ills of men and nations. Motilal Nehru's life was marked by an essential fidelity to civilization, by respect for human dignity and craving for human fellowship.

Motilal Nehru gave us a magnificent example of dignified, disciplined behaviour which we should remember whenever we enter the precincts of Parliament.

His life blended with the life of the country. After independence we have been trying to translate his ideals into effective reality. It will take us a long time before we can say that democracy is functioning here irrespective of caste, community, race and religion. But every one of us must look upon himself as a dedicated servant of that noble cause, which will lift us out of our own pusillanimity and make us worthy of a great cause, a modern civilized society.

His appearance reminded us of the ancient Roman consuls. He had a regal presence, a lordly manner and moved through the world on a high plane and dominated every gathering. He had not the taint of commonness but had a distinction in his manner.

He was a great lawyer, a great patriot, a great man, who was incapable of anything mean or dishonourable. His personal and powerful character won him esteem from both Indians and the British.

In every sense of the word, Motilal Nehru was a magnanimous man.

~

Indian culture has survived for nearly sixty centuries. Though it passed through many ups and downs, it has come down to us with its unfathomable depths and great capacity for devotion and service. What constitutes the national spirit or genius springs from deep and ancient, all the time diverting and altering their course, now in flood but on occasions parched and dry. These are the imponderables that bring history home to our consciousness and make facts look stranger than fiction. We have suffered defeat on many occasions. These misfortunes have not broken our spirit. After every blow, India found herself again, and made advances in spite of pain and sorrow.

Today, we are in one of the creative epochs of our history. We are trying our best to remould our heritage with insight into the profundities and with awareness of the demands of our age. Motilal was not a victim of the blind fatality of history in a violent age. He had faith in the spirit of man to mould history.

References

1 Among the notable members of the All-Parties Committee, apart from Motilal Nehru as Chairman wee: Sir Ali Imam, Tej Bahadur Sapru and Subhas Bose. The Committee submitted its report in August 1929 which *The Hindustan Times* in its editorial hailed it as '...Magna Carta of our liberty' but was rejected by the Muslim League in the absence of separate electorate for Muslims.

2 Skeen Committee was appointed in June 1925 under Lt Gen Andrew Skeen with one British member and 11 Indian members to study the feasibility of establishing military colleges in India to train officers for the Indian Army.

3 Swaraj Party was formed by C.R. Das as a result of his differences with Gandhi on Non-cooperation Movement.

4 A statutory commission led by Sir John Simon, to investigate the working of Montague-Chelmsford Reforms, which were a 'half-way house' to responsible government in which all important subjects were reserved for the Governor-General's discretion, while unimportant subjects were transferred to local government.

5 A mass non-violent movement under the leadership of Mahatma Gandhi, denying the legitimacy of the British rule and refusing to pay taxes.

'Men like Lajpat Rai cannot die as long as sun shines in the Indian sky.'
— Mahatma Gandhi

NINE

Lala Lajpat Rai

(Jan 28, 1865 – Nov 17, 1928)

Lala Lajpat Rai, or Lalaji as he was respectfully called, was popularly also referred to as *Punjab Kesri* 'the Lion of the Punjab'. He was one of the legendary triumvirate — Lal-Bal-Pal[1] — of India's freedom movement and dedicated his life to selfless service for the country.

There is hardly any other leader with the exception of Gandhi whose public activities covered such a wide range as Lalaji. As Gandhi himself put it, 'It is impossible to think of a single public movement in which Lalaji was not to be found'.

~

Lajpat Rai started his life as a lawyer at Hissar and then moved to Lahore where he built up considerable prestige and a lucrative practice at the Bar.

He was disturbed by many of the pernicious social practices and forms which had crept into the Hindu faith and wished to free society from these social evils. He recognized that until political freedom was won it would not be easy to rid the society of the grave disabilities from which many of its members, especially the women, suffered.

He, therefore, turned to politics to affect the change and became an ardent fighter for political freedom and a courageous crusader against caste, untouchability and the subjection of women.

~

He looked at education as a powerful instrument for achieving social and national progress and was drawn into one of the most creative movements of modern India — Arya Samaj, founded and led by Swami Dayanand Saraswati. He was one of the founding members of DAV College Managing Committee which in 1885 set up DAV School, Lahore, later upgraded to College.

In a newspaper[2] article written as early as 1901 he made a strong appeal for technical and industrial education but it was with the success of Swadeshi Movement (anti-partition movement of Bengal 1905-08) and the Non-Cooperation Movement[3] that 'the idea of national education caught imagination of the country'. Two nationalist educational institutions were set up and Lala Lajpat Rai was the moving force behind one of them – the National College, Lahore in 1921 (the other one was Jamia Millia in Delhi). It produced a number of students who contributed to freedom struggle, most prominent of them being Bhagat Singh and Sukhdev, who were later hanged in the Saunders' murder case.

I recall when I was a student we were deeply disturbed and agitated by the arrests and without trial deportations of Lala Lajpat Rai and Sardar Ajit Singh[4] in May 1907 for protesting against unfair against higher land revenue and increased irrigation rates in Punjab.

One contemporary British report pointed out. 'The head and centre of the entire movement is Lajpat Rai, a *khatri* pleader. He is a revolutionary and a political enthusiast who is inspired by the most intense hatred of the British Government'.

In 1914 he gave up his law practice and dedicated his life to fighting for freedom of the Motherland. He travelled to England and the United States to promote the cause of freedom and founded The Indian Home Rule League of America in New York. Besides travelling from coast-to-coast lecturing on the Indian situation, he authored *England's Debt to India* summarizing the disastrous consequences of English economic policies on India.

On his return from the United States in 1920, grateful countrymen invited him to preside over a special session of the Indian National Congress at Calcutta[5] where non-cooperation movement was launched against the foreign rule. He joined the Swaraj Party[6] founded by Motilal Nehru, C.R. Das and others, and was elected to the Central Assembly.

Later in the 1920s I had the honour of meeting Lala Lajpat Rai at Pandit Madan Mohan Malaviya's house in Banaras and also saw him at work in the Central Assembly as a member of the Swaraj Party under Pandit Motilal Nehru's leadership. This was just a few years before his death.

'India is neither Hindu nor Muslim,
not even both. It is one. It is India.'

Lala Lajpat Rai

Under his leadership the Central Legislative Assembly of Punjab passed a resolution advocating the boycott of the Simon Commission[7]. He followed up on the resolution by his personal example. When the Simon Commission actually arrived in Lahore in 1928, he led a procession expressing India's resentment against the Commission. The police dispersed the crowd with brutal *lathi*-charges and Lajpat Rai was fatally injured. He never recovered and passed away on November 17, 1928.

Many members of the Swaraj Party were not quite sympathetic to Gandhi's methods of civil disobedience and non-violent non-cooperation for gaining political freedom. In the first issue of *The People*[8], Lajpat Rai's differences with Gandhi's programme were expressed clearly. He wrote:

> 'Melodrama and an excessive sentimentality have no place in politics. For some time we have been busy making experiments with schemes which could not possibly be carried out without an immediate radical change in human nature.
>
> Politics deals primarily and essentially with the facts of a nation's life and the possibilities of its progress in the light of these. Human nature cannot be changed in months and years. You may require decades, even centuries, for that.
>
> Prophets and dreamers and visionaries are the salt of the earth. The world would be much poorer without them. But a campaign of political emancipation of a nation under foreign rule imposed and maintained at the point of the bayonet cannot be based on an attempt to change human nature quickly. Such attempts are bound to fail and end in disastrous action.'

Lajpat Rai did not live to see the fruition of Gandhi's attempt to win freedom by peaceful methods.

~

At times like the present, when in different parts of the world there are wars and piling up of nuclear armaments, it is wise to remember that there is no other way for the safety of the world than that taught by Gandhi.

We may suffer but we should not inflict suffering on others. International conflicts can be resolved by peaceful methods only if we have the will, the patience and the necessary forbearance to achieve peace and harmony between nations. It is true that moments may come when human nature feels justified in meeting one wrong with another. But our recent history is a living protest against any such precipitate action.

Even though Lajpat Rai did everything in his power to fight discrimination among the people, we still discriminate in the name of caste or community, race or religion. These hurt the pride of those who are discriminated against and Lajpat Rai was greatly disturbed by these discriminating activities. He was a firm believer in social equality.

If there is any lesson which we have to learn from the life and work of Lajpat Rai, it is that political stability can be based only on social equality. We have to carry out the fight against inequalities imposed on us by force of custom or authority of the past. Lajpat Rai's burning patriotism, his capacity to take risks and submit to suffer, his exile to Britain and America, his deportation and martyrdom, showed the stuff of which he was made.

As a visionary and a man with a mission, he was actively involved with the birth, growth and evolution of Punjab National Bank in its founding years. He also founded Lakshmi Insurance Company, Servants of People Society[9] and a chest hospital in Lahore.

All his life he lived like a hero and in death too he was crowned a martyr.

Paying a touching tribute to Lajpat Rai Gandhi feelingly wrote in *Young India*[10] of November 22, 1928: 'Men like Lajpat Rai cannot die as long as the sun shines in the Indian sky.'

References

1 Lal-Bal-Pal: Lala Lajpat Rai, Bal Gangadhar Tilak and Bipin Chandra Pal.

2 *Kayastha Samachar* was an Urdu monthly which in 1899 converted to English.

3 In 1920, Gandhi started the Non-Cooperation Movement and urged everyone to quit government jobs and boycott government educational institutions.

4 Sardar Ajit Singh (1881-1947): Popularly known as the hero of *Pagdi Sambhal Jatta* movement, founded the underground 'Bharat Mata Society' (*Mehboobe-Watan* in Urdu), to reignite the 1857 rebellion on its 50th anniversary in 1907.

Such was the popularity of this movement that many Sikh soldiers refused to obey British orders to fire on farmer rallies. Fearing increase in revolutionary activities both Ajit Singh and Lajpat Rai were arrested and sent to Mandalay Jail in Burma. While Congress pleaded for Lalaji's release it maintained complete silence on Ajit Singh. However, fearing the spread of Pagdi Sambhal Jatta movement among the entire army Ajit Singh was also released.

5 Special session of the Indian National Congress at Calcutta.

6 Swaraj Party or the Congress Khilafat Party was formed on Jan. 1, 1923 by C.R. Das and Motilal Nehru.

[7] Simon Commission: A seven member British parliamentary delegation led by Sir John Simon come to India to study and suggest constitutional reforms. Both Congress and Muslim League boycotted it because it had no Indian member.

[8] Weekly newspaper from Lahore edited by Lala Lajpat Rai. It became popular due to Lalaji's candid views and fearless political comments.

[9] Servants of People Society was started by Lala Lajpat Rai in 1921 in Lahore. The object of the Society was to enlist and train national missionaries for service of the Motherland. After independence, the society shifted to Delhi.

[10] Young India.

A world citizen: A viswa-manava.

TEN

Rabindranath Tagore

(May 7, 1861 – Aug 7, 1941)

In the preface to his collected works, Rabindranath says, 'This world I have loved; Greatness I have saluted; Freedom I have aspired for and I have believed that Man is true and that Universal Man is ever living in the heart of the people.'

~

Rabindranath Tagore raised the stature of our country in the eyes of the world. He was a versatile genius, a literary artist, an educator, a composer, a singer, an actor. Nature was liberal to him in her gifts and fortune in her favours. His outlook was based not on knowledge but on vision.

Rabindranath did not give us a system of philosophy but gave us flashes of light which illumine our minds and warm our hearts. His work does not so much convey a message as embody a vision. To lift man out of the stale air of common life, to regions where the eternal verities are seen undimmed by self or sophistry and man's ordinary existence becomes a life, a passion, a power, this was Rabindranath's life-mission.

A man of genius is said to be a compound of the qualities of a man, woman, and a child, of vigour, of intellect, intensity of feeling and the perpetual wonder of a child. All of us have in some degree the sense of curiosity, of wonder.

Rabindranath pleaded not only for concord with the past, but also for freedom from the past. All healthy growth needs continuity and change. We are not free unless our minds are liberated from dead forms, tyrannical restrictions and crippling social habits. Every fresh movement of spirit means the casting off of the old body, of the garments. Rabindranath felt that the Indian people were much too self-centered and lazy in their minds to get over prejudices.

While a stagnant pool breeds malaria and mosquitoes, a living current cleanses its waters as it hurries along. Perpetual renewal and rededication to self-development are the essence of life.

He asks us to measure ourselves against the achievements of our forefathers. Streams of men poured into the country in resistless tides from places unknown and were lost in the one single sea of India. Aryans and Dravidians, Sakas and Huns, Pathans and Moghuls, these people of diverse origin influenced Indian culture which is one, though varied in its manifestations.

Through these tumultuous ages, says Tagore, India has saved the living words that have issued from the illumined consciousness of her great seers. The genius of a few has touched the hearts of many.

The urgent need of the human race is to move a step forward in its evolution. Rabindranath's mission was one of reconciliation between East and West in a spirit of understanding and mutual enlightenment. 'All humanity's greatness is mine. The infinite personality of man can only come from the magnificent harmony of all human races.

My prayer is that India may represent the co-operation of all the people on this earth. For India unity is truth, and division is evil.'

~

In his *Religion of Man* he writes: 'I do not consider India to be a geographical entity. To me it is a spiritual personality. This is the spirit of faith in the metaphysical being of man which may perhaps exhaust all our material prosperity. Even after losing everything India stands steadfastly embracing that spirit. It is a glory sufficient to justify hope for its future.'

In 1925, he brought out a book, *The Geographical Introduction to History*: 'There can be no play without a stage, no history without geography. Historical consciousness is revived in peoples' memories by association with certain places.'

'To know my country, one has to travel to that age when she realized her soul and thus transcended her physical boundaries, when she revealed her being in a radiant magnanimity which illumined the eastern horizon, making her recognized as their own by those in alien shores who were awakened into a surprise of life, and not now when she has withdrawn herself into a narrow barrier of obscurity, into a misery of pride, of exclusiveness, into a poverty of mind that dumbly revolves around itself in an unmeaning repetition of a past that has lost its sight and has no message for the pilgrim of the future.

Rabindranath's prayer for his country is, 'Let the promises and hopes, the deeds and words of my country be true, my Lord.' He does not say 'my country, right or wrong' but prays that his country may always adopt the right line of conduct.

~

He did not live in an ivory tower. He was born at a time when India was in a revolutionary mood. There was a conscious revolt against social, political and religious institutions.

Though Rabindranath was essentially a literary artist, his voice was raised whenever grave injustices were committed. When evil is perpetrated, we have an obligation to speak out and act against it. Tagore, along with Gandhi, was responsible for the awakening of the national spirit and was as much against the cowardice of the weak as against the arrogance of the strong. In his patriotism there was no trace of hatred, bitterness or chauvinism.

He believed that political development was inseparable from moral development. Our political bondage was a symptom of our inward weakness. 'They who have failed to attain *Swaraj* within themselves must lose it in the outside world too.'

He demanded a positive programme of national reconstruction and not a mere rejection of foreign rule. We must remove the internal causes which give rise to social and political instability.

When the Sedition Bill[1] was passed in 1898 and the great leader Tilak was arrested, Tagore raised his voice against the repressive policy of the Government and actively participated in raising funds for Tilak's defence.

When Bengal was partitoned in 1905[2], Tagore was greatly disturbed. He poured out songs full of the spirit of nationalism. 'There is no salvation for man if the power of the weak is not awakened at once, because the weapon of the powerful has exceeded its limits; the helplessness of the weak knows no bounds today; all opportunities and advantages are heaped on one side of human society while helplessness reigns supreme on the other.'

When the Jallianwala Bagh[3] attrocities occurred, he returned his knighthood and wrote a letter to the Viceroy, Lord Chelmsford, which concluded with the words, 'The time has come when badges of honour make our shame glaring in their incongruous context of distinctions, by the side of those of my countrymen who, for their so-called insignificance, are liable to suffer a degradation not fit for human beings.'

There was a conscious revolt against social, political and religious institutions. Rabindranath participated in this movement and helped it forward. While he was aware of the social inadequacy and religious reaction and protested against them, he was deeply convinced of the validity and vitality of the fundamental ideals set forth by the seers and saints of India:

O Motherland! in thee the whole world takes delight.
First from thy forest-dwellings rose the sacred songs;
First from thy dawning spread the light
Of noble thoughts and deeds, in epic verses told.

Rabindranath's poetry became future of India's history; *Jana Gana Mana* was sung for the first time at the Calcutta session of the Indian National Congress in 1911. It became our National Anthem. It is a song in praise of the land with its hills and rivers, and with its many peoples, races and religions, all woven in a garland of love. It is a stirring appeal to unity under the Creator, the Dispenser of India's destiny, *bharata-bhagya-vidhātā*. The words kindle in the heart of man, the sense of unity of oneself with all and bring the hearts of all people into the harmony of one life.

Tagore's nationalism did not exclude internationalism. In a poem entitled *Pravasi* (The Emigrant) he writes:

> My home is everywhere;
> I am in search of it;
> My country is in all countries;
> I will struggle to attain it.

The Second World War disturbed him a great deal. When Miss Eleanor Rathbone[4] wrote 'An Open Letter to Indian Friends' to persuade India to come openly into the war against the Nazi Germany, he pointed out how India herself had no political freedom.

In his reply written from his deathbed he eloquently wrote:

> It is not that the British are foreigners that they are unwelcome and have found no place in our hearts, as because, while pretending to be trustees for our welfare, they have betrayed the great trust and sacrificed the happiness of millions in India to bloat the pockets of a few at home.

> I should have thought that the decent Britisher would at least keep silent at these wrongs and be grateful to us for our inaction, but that she should add insult to injury, and pour salt over our wounds, passes all bounds of decency.

In his address on *The Crisis of Civilization,* which he wrote a few weeks before his death, Tagore asks us to crusade for a civilization in which peace would be possible. Only an ethical movement can rescue us from the spirit of barbarism which has corrupted our civilization and is breeding wars and more destructive wars.

Tagore rebelled against orthodoxies, clashes of castes and creeds and indifference to the disinherited of the earth.

> My head is bowed in sorrow
> My eyes keep back their tears
> My heart is rent by this reproach.

~

Indian tradition believes that man has to grow from the intellectual to the spiritual level. An intellectual apprehension of the Divine is different from the spiritual realization of it. 'Perfect freedom lies in the harmony of relationship which we realize not through knowing but in being.'

The ultimate truth in man is not his intellect but the illumined consciousness which he acquires when he extends his sympathy across all barriers of caste and colour. He then realizes that all things are spiritually alive. The world is not alien to us. It is the habitation of Man's spirit. Every object in existence has something ineffable about it.

The experience of Reality which the great seers have is not capable of exact definition. So varied representations are given. These are fashioned by heart, intelligence and mind — *hṛdā, manīṣā,* and *mānasa*, the *Upaniṣads* tell us.

> Not within the field of vision stands this form,
> no one whatsoever sees Him with the eye
> By heart, by thought, by mind apprehended,
> they who know Him become immortal.

In the name of spiritual freedom, we should not retreat from action. Austerity is not inaction. 'Thus we have come to know that what India truly seeks is that which is in *śivam* (God), in goodness which is in truth of perfect union; that India does not enjoin her children to cease from *Karma* (action) but to perform their karma in the presence of the Eternal, with the pure knowledge of the spiritual meaning of existence.

Asceticism for Rabindranath is self-control and not abstention from worldly activities.

> 'India has not split up her *dharma* by setting apart one side of it for practical and the other for ornamental purposes. *Dharma* in India is religion for the whole society — its roots reach deep underground, but its top touches the Heaven, overspreading the whole life of man, like a gigantic banyan tree.
>
> To realize the One in the universe and also in our own inner nature, to discover it by means of knowledge, to perceive it by means of love and to preach it by means of conduct — this is the work that India has been doing in spite of many obstacles and calamities, in ill success and good fortune alike.'

India has two aspects — in one she is a householder; in the other a wandering ascetic. The former refuses to budge from the home corner, the latter has no home at all. I find both these within me. I want to roam about and see all the wide world, yet I also yearn for a little sheltered nook; like a bird with its tiny nest for a dwelling, and the vast sky for flight.'

He has a sensitive social conscience. When he referred to the evil days on which the country had fallen, he emphasized the social inadequacies, the humiliations and hardships to which millions of our countrymen were subjected. We are all born equal but we are made unequal by the way we are brought up. Reverence for personality is the central principle of all ethics. In our practice we have overlooked it.

Rabindranath's religion is based on vision, experience rather than on knowledge.

The poet's religion has no place for any fixed doctrine. Religion is an endless adventure of man's entire being towards a truth which is revealed in this very quest. Truth is not the exclusive possession of any one individual or class or race or religion.

One Truth has many faces, *bahūni mukhāni ekam sat viprā bahudhā vadanti*.

The real is one; wise men speak of it in many ways. On the basis of such a view, India had been struggling for *sarva-dharma-samanvaya*.

The variations are determined by the accidents of geography and history. The concepts of God are relative to our traditions

Rabindranath's prayer for his country is, 'Let the promises and hopes, the deeds and words of my country be true, my Lord.' He does not say 'my country, right or wrong' but prays that his country may always adopt the right line of conduct.

and training. This emphasis on unity in diversity as against uniformity, has persisted for centuries in the Indian outlook. The latter view negates discord for unity, comprehends the differences. When differences become contradictions, conflicts arise.

Tagore repudiates narrow, dogmatic, exclusive views of religion. It is wrong to think that certain nations, certain races and certain creeds are specially chosen by God.

In his essay *on The Centre of Indian Culture*, Tagore says: 'We should remember that the doctrine of special creation is out of date, and the idea of a specially favoured race belongs to a barbaric age. We have come to understand that any special truth or special culture which is wholly dissociated from the universal is not true at all.'

He reminds us that, 'Our forefathers spread a single white carpet whereon all the world was cordially invited to take its seat in amity and good fellowship. No quarrel could have arisen there, for He in whose name the invitation went forth, for all time to come, was the Peaceful, in the heart of all conflicts; the God who is revealed through all losses and sufferings; the One in all diversities of creation. And in His name was this eternal truth declared in ancient India. He alone sees, who sees all beings in himself.'

'God,' Rabindranath says, 'has many strings to his *sitar*; some are made of iron, others of copper, and yet others are made of gold. Humanity is the golden string of God's lute. His freedom, his ethical and aesthetic consciousness make man the golden string.'

For Tagore, God, man and nature are bound together in single unity.

For Tagore the whole universe is a manifestation of the Supreme, *īśā vāsyam idaṁ sarvaṁ*. All things are interrelated in God, *sūtre maṇi-gaṇā iva*. Spirit and life are two poles of one Reality. When the world is enveloped by God, its pettiness is relieved. Tagore agrees with Pascal who says that 'a man does not show his greatness by being at one extremity, but rather by touching both at once.'

Religion is not to be confused with doctrinal conformity or ceremonial piety. It is the purification of the soul, the remaking of self. It is not a mere quest of truth but a conquest of our selfishness, pride, greed, etc. It is through self-control that man can reach his goal. The extinction of the ego is the way to fulfilment. Progress towards the goal is through continual sacrifice. 'Life,' says Rabindranath, 'is an eternal sacrifice at the altar of death.'

Religion, if it is not to fade away, should undergo a radical transformation. Ancient dogmas do not touch our hearts or satisfy our minds. Forms that were adapted to situations and issues that no longer exist require to be changed. Our doubts have dimensions deeper than we realize.

Rabindranath understands the doubts and difficulties felt by the critics of religion. Atheism is not a negative denial of God but a positive movement of the spirit to reach the Divine behind the new dimensions of reality which modern knowledge provides. Though knowledge has no limit, mystery has no end.

'I am able to love my God because He gives me freedom to deny Him.'

Dissatisfaction with the actual and yearning for the Beyond are the keynote of all religions. Man struggles to attain perfection. To fail to achieve it is no disgrace; to lack the desire for it is a misfortune. Man's struggle is for emancipation.

I am restless. I am a thirst for far away things,
My soul goes out in a longing to touch the skirt of
the dim distance.

O Great Beyond, O the keen call of thy flute!

I forget, I ever forget, that I have no wings to fly, that I
am bound in this spot evermore.

~

He was not only a poet and a playwright but a novelist and a story teller, a composer and an actor, a serious thinker and a social reformer, an educator, a nationalist and an internationalist.

He has given innocent joy to many children by his stories like *Kabuliwalah*. He gathered fragments of moonlight and distilled them into words as in his *Crescent Moon*.

He was sensitive to the beauty of women. In his poem *The Bridegroom*, he says:

Because you and I shall meet
    The heavens are full of light,
Because you and I shall meet
    The world is full of greenery.

He sang of beauty and heroism, nobility and charm, resignation and despair, the fervour of revolt and the shame of defeat. When we read this great poet, we see the world with rechristened eyes. 'My heart throbs to mingle with the heart of humanity. Some seek wisdom, others seek wealth, but I seek the company so that I may sing.' Tagore does not believe in a sheltered life. In one of his poems in *Gitanjali* he says: 'Our

Master Himself has joyfully taken upon Him the bonds of creations. He is bound with us all forever.'

His songs are sung not only in Bengal but all over the country.

Rabindranath's great works sprang from intensity of vision and feeling. In his literary works he spoke of that province of human life, vast and boundless, with its affections and sympathies, loves and friendships, joys and sorrows of which mere intellect does not speak.

Though his work was rooted in Indian soil his mind ranged over the wide world and his knowledge of human nature was deep. His work has, therefore, a universal appeal. His poems and songs vibrate with a peculiar passion which the pursuit of beauty aroused in him. They speak of the vicissitudes of friendship, the beauty of love, the pain of desolation, laughter and tears, terror and delight, the vanity of human wishes, the pains and heartaches of unfulfilled desires, the horror of moral obliquity, the shame of infamous conduct. They have the power of stirring our deepest emotions.

Rabindranath's writings have been translated into many languages but even the best translations do not bring out the music and the melody, the fire and the force of the original.

The philosophic outlook of India inspired the writings of Rabindranath Tagore. Philosophy had no place in the original family of the Muses. Coleridge[5], however, considered it to be a twin genius to Poetry. While discussing Shakespeare's Poetry, Coleridge says: 'No man was ever yet a great poet without being at the same time a profound philosopher.'

We find in Rabindranath the conjunction of a brilliant imagination and a passionate concern for conveying through his writings the basic intellectual and moral concepts of Indian culture. All ages of renaissance are ages when men suddenly discover the seed of thought in their ancient past. Rabindranath says: 'Emancipation from the bondage of the soil is no freedom for the tree.'

In *A Poet's Testament*, Rabindranath confesses: 'I have completed seventy years of my life but even now my friends complain of the trait of frivolity which interferes with the gravity becoming to old age. I am afraid I cannot afford to be more serious. Those who want to place me on a high pedestal, with the ringing of bells and the sounding of conchshells, to them I would say, "I have been born in a lower rung...I am a poet and nothing else".'

As if these activities were not enough, he turned to painting towards the end of his life. He rejected traditional canons and experimented with new forms and colour compositions. His paintings and sketches — more than 1500 of them are preserved — take us to the realm of the fantastic and the unreal.

~

Tagore's philosophy was one of wholeness and unity. He fought against the evil of division, of multiplicity.

India's history is not a separate exclusive history of either the Hindus or the Muslims. 'Those Muslims,' Rabindranath said, 'who throughout the ages and since so many generations had made the soil of this land their own, by births and deaths — they too have a place in the history of India.' Even the British have become a part of our history.

~

We honour him not only for this many-sided genius but also for the guidance of his life and work in this troubled world.

There is something in Rabindranath's teaching that is not of this earth. He was concerned with the invisible spirit of man, with the profundities and not the trivialities of life. He asks us to cling to ultimate common sense in the confusion of life. He believed in regeneration through love and suffering. He was not afraid of change.

Genius is distant vision: *dūra dṛṣṭi*; it is anticipating experience. Rabindranath felt the destiny of the world as a fellowship of people. His Visva-Bharati was a world university, a preparation for the distant goal where the world makes a home in a single nest: *yatra visvam bhavati ekanidam*. All races and nations belong to the one world. A commonwealth of mind and spirit is a prelude to a political commonwealth. Tagore was a world citizen: a *viśva-mānava*.

He built a monument for himself not merely as a record of achievements but also as a lesson to posterity. The world claims him as its own because of what he became, and what millions of human beings hunger to become. He attained that perfect co-ordination of being that belongs to genius, that serenity of mind sought by many and achieved by few.

His songs are sung and his verses are remembered. His voice was the conscience of our age. He became a spokesman and a guide for his generation. He bequeathed to his country and the world, a life which had no littleness about it.

References

[1] Sedition Bill 1898 was introduced by the British as part of their efforts to curb criticism of the colonial government and to stamp out all forms of dissent.

[2] Under the recommendation of Lord Curzon, Bengal was divided in 1905, creating a new province of East Bengal.

[3] A walled garden in Amritsar, where people celebrating the festival of Baisakh on April 13, 1919, were continuously fired upon by troops on the orders of Brigadier General R.E.H Dyer, killing 379 persons and wounding 1200, including women and children.

[4] Eleanor Florence Rathbone was an independent British member of parliament.

[5] Samuel Taylor Coleridge was an English poet, philosopher, and literary critic. Along with William Wordsworth he was the founder of Romantic Movement in England.

A courageous rebel, a wise statesman and a model administrator.

ELEVEN

Sardar Vallabhbhai Patel

(Oct 31, 1875 – Dec 15, 1950)

Sardar Patel was a man of great courage, a patriot and a man of great sagacious wisdom. We may look upon his life in three parts — a rebel, a statesman and an administrator.

During the struggle for independence he remained a loyal lieutenant of the Mahatma — Gandhi's word was the law to him. Like a disciplined soldier carrying out the behests of his leader he carried out Mahatma's wishes. Even when he differed, he subordinated his personal inclinations to the decisions of his leader whose mandate he was carrying out. In whatever he did, he carried out the wishes of Gandhi.

Under Gandhi's guidance he conducted the Civil Resistance campaigns in Borsad and Bardoli. He asked the peasants of Bardoli to challenge the Government to confiscate and take their lands to England. Bardoli became the sign of hope and symbol of strength of the Indian peasants. Not only in Borsad and Bardoli, but in several other battles of freedom, he was in the front rank. Everywhere he acted with great discipline. He never put his own interests higher than those of the nation.

Observing his work in Bardoli, on June 3, 1928 Gandhi wrote in his letter, 'the battle for Bardoli is going on very well. Long live Sardar to fight many a good fight.'

Later he remarked: 'Vallabhbhai found his Vallabh (God) in Bardoli.'

The campaigns which he organized were all intended to bring together the people of the areas concerned, to bind them together, and to get them to subordinate their caste and communal differences and function as one whole; to have them work towards one single purpose. That task yet requires to be completed.

~

The most important contribution of his life's work was as a statesman. Patel realized that the political stability of the country depended on its unity. Immediately after independence, in a period of two years, he integrated over 500 states into the Indian Union. By bringing the 500 and odd states into the framework of Central administration he integrated India into one country.

Through his persuasive power, diplomatic skill, political adroitness, he was able to bring about administrative unity of this country, which was an essential base for building a strong India.

As Prime Minister Nehru said, 'Sardar Patel is the architect of India's unity.'

How smoothly he accomplished this task is illustrated by the fact that the Maharaja of Gwalior, who was himself affected by this process of integration, later paid rich tributes to the vision and work of Sardar Patel.

The state of this country without the remarkable national unity that Sardar achieved is hard to imagine. Even after coming together as one nation, we are still asking for integration and solidarity. Look around at the provinces, at different parts of the country — you will find that communal differences, caste animosities, and other such divisive issues continue to dominate our public affairs. Distinctions such as Kamma and Reddy, Lingayat and Vokkaligars, Kayasth and Rajput — these differences still influence our public life.

Our history in recent times has been marred by the exaggerated attachment we give to these things. We must look upon ourselves as Indians first and foremost. The countries which have made the greatest progress in the East are Japan and China. There are Christians living there, there are Buddhists and there are Muslims; but no one thinks of their personal interests when the interests of the nation are involved. Everyone looks upon himself as Japanese or a Chinese. Here in our country we still regard ourselves as belonging to one community or a caste and these differences dominate, vitiate and pollute our social structure.

The national unification Sardar Patel achieved has still to be transformed into emotional integration and national cohesion. For years we have been trying for this national cohesion. What is needed is a complete integration of our country. We may belong to any caste or any religion; but that must be regarded as a very subordinate aspect and purely a personal matter of the individual. These should not be brought into public life.

Anyone who encourages fissiparous tendencies is no friend of the country. We must develop social solidarity which transcends the bonds of kinship, caste and religion.

It is, therefore, essential that the integration of the country which Sardar started must be continued till we all feel that we belong to one nation. That is the integration which we are still aiming at.

About the achievement of Sardar in this matter, I recall a comment made by The London Times when Sardar died —

'This (unification of India) will stand out as a great historic achievement by Sardar Patel on level with Bismarck, if not higher.'

He had a job to do and he did it.

~

I remember that three of our great leaders were at one time Chairmen of three different municipalities, or corporations as they are called today. Rajen Babu* was the Chairman of Patna Municipality; Jawaharlal Nehru was Chairman of Allahabad Municipality; and Sardar Patel was Chairman of Ahmedabad Municipality. Their selfless labour and their organizing skill were known to all and are still recalled by people.

As Chairman of the Ahmedabad Municipality, Sardar Patel transformed it into a modern public service body. People did not talk of leakage and wastage of public funds. They were sure that everything collected would be usefully spent for the purpose for which it was intended. Today, there is much talk of corruption

---

* Dr. Rajendra Prasad who was elected the First President of India in 1950.

'This (unification of India) will stand out as a great historic achievement by Sardar Patel on level with Bismarck, if not higher.'

The London Times

in public life, which may be true or may not be true. But that there should be such talk is a reflection on our general character, morality and ability of the administrators.

As administrators we therefore, must see to it that our actions and words leave no room or scope for criticism of any type.

Sardar was a man of few words. He possessed clarity of thought, conviction and prudence. This made him successful in implementing his ideas; in any Committee one who knows his mind will always prevail over others who approach the problems with unstructured thinking or blank minds. He always knew what he wanted to accomplish and accomplished it. Firmness and decisiveness were his characteristics.

As an administrator he quickly responded to the needs of the people and demonstrated great organizational skill in responding to their concerns adequately. In 1922 when Borsad suffered the dual tyranny of dacoits and 'punitive taxation' in his capacity as a lawyer Sardar Patel directed the residents not to pay the 'punitive tax' compelling the British government to withdraw the tax.

When Bardoli suffered floods and famine in 1926 and the Bombay Presidency raised taxes to 30%, Patel organised the farmers to stop paying taxes. Though non-compliance meant possible confiscation of properties and prison, the farmers agreed. The tax was finally revoked in 1928.

One of Patel's key achievements was creating cohesion and building trust amongst different castes and communities which were divided on socio-economic lines.

People who administer a great nation like ours must demonstrate ability to stay in touch with the people and to organize quick corrective action; they must be above suspicion, must be able to risk their lives, and if necessary, for the sake of the country and not pander to the whims or the pressures of society. That is very necessary.

~

Having achieved freedom and administrative unification, something more needs to be done if our country is to become a first-class power, and not remain a second-class or a third-class power: complete cohesion and integration, subordination of our minor differences to the one great concept of India as a living part of humanity.

In the Independence pledge it is said that the British brought on us a four-fold disaster — political, economic, cultural and spiritual. Now when control over the country is in our hands, these four unhappy consequences of foreign rule need to be eliminated.

The economic standards will have to be raised. Unless we can get rid of the demon of poverty, unless we are able to bring down hunger, unemployment and disease, we will not be able to raise the economic standards of our people. It is the low economic standards which are ultimately responsible for caste and communal differences. The root cause of all our troubles — caste trouble, communal trouble, low caste and Harijan issues and untouchablity — can ultimately be traced to the extreme poverty from which most of our people suffer.

If we are able to raise the living standards of our people, this suffering will not continue. Not only better standards of living but accepting that each individual is a keystone in the arch of a great country is critical. Our people are the most valuable asset which we possess, and unless we are able to give them some kind of cultural outlook, a sense of belonging to a great nation with great traditions; in no sense can our education be regarded as complete.

People generally say that they do not believe in religion. There is skepticism in matters of belief; there exists a lack of morality and sense of values. Religion is not something which is an aside or a parenthesis. It is the deepest part of our being. The Infinite or Supreme is the deepest part of our being. We must work not on the surface but from our ultimate depths. Life from depth is an authentic religious life.

In all our activities, if we observe a sense of values from our inner individual depths, we will be religious. If we are able to give to our children that kind of outlook, they will not be carried away by the sophistications and the skepticism of the modern world. We will really become a deeply authentic and moral in the true sense of the word.

A living and vibrant democracy with strong moral values to bind the democracy, raising of the living standards of our people, giving a proper cultural outlook to our young men and women as also a sense of oneness in their relationship with neighbours — that is what we must aim at; and it is my earnest hope that in this country we will soon have this proper orientation.

~

Like all great men of history, Sardar could be angry though he rarely lost his temper. He was never self-righteous. He had no personal fads or conventional prejudices. He had an acute sense of the past; a critical appreciation of what in our history and traditions had vitality and power of survival. Life must be understood backwards and lived forwards. We should not cling to the past. In politics, as in life, it is silly to cry for last month's moon.

He was one of the pivotal figures in our recent history both before and after the achievement of freedom.

Revolutions generally leave a trail of disappointment and disillusionment behind them. In the excitement of the struggle we proclaim great ideals and entertain high hopes. When the struggle is over and in the face of hard realities we attempt to apply the ideals which guided the struggle, there are compromises and retreats which tarnish the purity of the achievement. Every successful revolution faces criticism not only from its dispossessed victims, but also from its one-time supporters who accuse it of having betrayed its principles.

What is essential is adherence to discipline and fundamental ideals, ideas and principles which governed the revolution.

Life of Sardar Patel reminds us of the self-sacrificing labours of one of the great makers of modern India. His devotion to duty, his disciplined obedience, his courage and his willingness to throw away his life — these are all qualities which we have to learn from his example.

His life and accomplishments continue to emphasize and reiterate that freedom has to be continually re-earned by service and sacrifice.

In Sardar Vallabhbhai Patel we had a great courageous rebel, a wise statesman and a model administrator. If we remember these qualities of Sardar, our country will progress steadily.

It is my earnest hope that these great qualities of his will continue to inspire us in building a great future for this country.

Embodiment of that what is best in Indian culture.

TWELVE

Dr. Rajendra Prasad

(Dec 3, 1884 – Feb 28, 1963)

It is the good fortune of this country that in the formative years of our Republic, Dr. Prasad was elected President and that he guided the destiny of our country for over 12 years. As the first President of India for two continuous terms he adorned this place of highest honour and authority with rare distinction. He set the standards for correct constitutional behaviour.

He was the embodiment of what is best in Indian culture; the qualities of service, renunciation and sacrifice. It is these qualities which lead us to the peaks of our achievement. His life, from the time he entered the national struggle down to the last day of his life, was devoted to the service of this country.

Dr Rajendra Prasad along with Jawaharlal Nehru and Sardar Patel constituted the holy trinity that characterized the Gandhian leadership of the freedom struggle. The trio also nurtured the nascent nation with care, zeal and dexterity as the true heirs of the Mahatma.

Honours and positions were bestowed on him without his ever aspiring for them. As President of the Constituent Assembly he displayed admirable deftness, innate calmness and profound wisdom and accomplished the task to complete satisfaction of every section of the Constitution drafting body. No wonder, on attaining Independence he became the unanimous choice for the office of the President of India.[1]

As the first Head of the State, Rajen Babu, as was he respectfully addressed, not only lent dignity and grace to the exalted highest office of the land but also exercised a moderating influence on the policies and actions of the Government.

To a great extent the credit for success of the democratic system that has come to stay in India goes to leaders like Dr Rajendra Prasad who ably steered the nation during its formative and most crucial period. He, along with Nehru, was responsible for sowing the seeds of our Parliament polity — seeds in the form of precedents, conventions and traditions; of giving equal respect and consideration to the views of the opposition.

What exists today in the name of democracy cannot be regarded as satisfactory. Democracy is something which is perpetually responding to the changing aspirations of the people and times, moving forward; if it is not responsive, it is not democracy.

~

It is true that he took a leading part in many other activities. But here we are concerned with his work for the development of the Constitution and the work which he did for human fellowship.

Dr. Rajendra Prasad, as a faithful disciple of Gandhi, forcefully argued for equality and human fellowship — values which were later inscribed in our Constitution. That we, as a nation, stand for political justice and freedom, fraternity and fellowship is one of the remarkable principles enshrined in our Constitution. Many of the things that we do may appear to be not relevant and the objectives not achievable from a practical point of view but ultimately these small steps push us towards the objectives which seem impossible but finally will make the world a place in which we can live with amity and friendship.

In his first address on December 11, 1946 to the Constituent Assembly on being elected as its Permanent Chairman he said,[2]

> 'I am aware that this Constituent Assembly has been born with certain limitations placed on it from its very birth. We may not forget, disregard or ignore those limitations in arriving at our decisions. But I know that in spite of those limitations the Assembly is self-governing, proceedings of which no outside authority can interfere, and the decisions of which no one else outside it can upset or alter or modify.
>
> 'I hope you, Ladies and Gentlemen, who have come here for framing the constitution for an independent and free India, will be able to get rid of those limitations and place before the world a model of a constitution that will satisfy all our people — all groups, all communities, all religions — inhabiting this vast land, and which will ensure to everyone freedom of action, freedom of thought, freedom of belief and freedom of

worship; which will guarantee to everyone opportunities for rising to his highest, and which will guarantee to everyone freedom in all respects.

There is no reason why we also should not succeed (in our endeavours).

All that we need is honesty of purpose; firmness of determination; a desire to understand each other's view-point; to do justice, to behave as fairly and squarely as possible towards everyone else — with that determination, with that resolve, I cannot see why we should not be able to overcome the obstacles in our way.'[3]

~

The arrival of Mahatma Gandhi on the Indian national scene greatly influenced Dr. Prasad. Initially, he was not impressed with Gandhi's appearance or manner of conversation. In time, however, he was deeply moved by the dedication, conviction and courage that the Mahatma displayed and changed many of his views. He reduced the number of servants he had to one, and sought ways to simplify his life. He no longer felt shame in sweeping the floor, or washing his own utensils, tasks he had all along assumed others would do for him. He gave up his law practice and dedicated himself to freedom struggle.

In 1921 to uphold Swadeshi ideals he started National College in Patna.

As part of Gandhi's non-cooperation movement he called for non-cooperation in Bihar. The movement spread like wildfire. Machinery of the British Raj came to a grinding halt. Mass arrests and deployment of brutal force followed. In Chauri

Dr Rajendra Prasad embodied the finer values of service, dedication and modesty. Endowed with outstanding qualities of head and heart, he shaped the destiny of this nation for about 12 years.

Chaura[4] the peaceful non-cooperation turned violent. Gandhi suspended the civil disobedience movement. The entire nation was taken aback. A murmur of dissent began within the top brass of the Congress, but Rajen Babu stood by his mentor, seeing the wisdom behind the decision. Gandhi did not want to set a precedent of violence for free India.

His service on the various fronts of the movement for independence raised his profile considerably. He presided over the Bombay session of the Indian National Congress in October 1934 and was elected its President.

Rabindranath Tagore wrote to Dr. Rajendra Prasad, 'I feel assured in my mind that your personality will help to soothe the injured souls and bring peace and unity into an atmosphere of mistrust and chaos…'

~

The last address he gave as President of India was in June 1962 while inaugurating the New Delhi Anti-nuclear Arms Convention. As a true Gandhian, he made a strong case for shunning every kind of violence, and instead argued for peace and friendship among nations. He called upon all countries to cease nuclear testing of weapons. Even though it may have appeared utopian when he formulated it, it is an ideal to which the world continues to look forward to.

Though not under any illusion that disarmament would happen in a single step, he emphasized it was the only way for the human civilization to survive and prosper.

> 'The future of humanity is at stake. Non-combatants or neutral nations are as much involved as combatant

nations. Not only the living but also many generations of those yet born are doomed to be afflicted with congenital physical and mental defects.

'Nuclear weapons, far from ensuring the triumph of one way of life or the other, only promise the extinction of life.

'It is being said that the only way to prevent another nuclear war is to develop an adequate nuclear deterrent. (But) even if deterrence succeeds, the mounting scale of expenditure on armaments resulting from the nuclear race, would impoverish the nations concerned and deprive mankind of much of the fruits of scientific advancement.

'If we feel ourselves unable to undertake and achieve this in a single step, let us at least make a move in the right direction by banning all nuclear tests and give humanity breathing space to think and adopt further steps to rid the world of fear, distrust and suspicion which lie at the root of all violence.'

The causes that cause wars must be removed. The causes are mutual fear, distrust, animosities and the feeling of insecurity among nations. If we are to survive in this world as peaceful nations, these causes have to be removed. We must think in a new paradigm.

Men must feel that humanity is one whole, irrespective of caste or community, class or race. They must try to widen the horizon of their understanding, advance in knowledge, grow in grace and feel that when one individual in one part of the country or the world suffers, all others do suffer.

It is this ideal that possessed Dr. Rajendra Prasad to put forward the proposal of total nuclear disarmament even though he was certain that many in his audience would not accept the rationale of it.

~

Rajendra Prasad was a true Indian both in appearance and personality. By his appearance and dress he represented an ordinary Indian or an Indian farmer. But his sensibilities combined with a broad outlook, sharp intelligence and quick grasp of the most intricate issues, distinguished him from others.

In 1962, after 12 years as President, Dr. Prasad retired with a monthly pension of just Rs. 1,100. In the same year he was awarded the Bharat Ratna. During the Sino-India war he donated his wife's jewellery to Indian treasury.

He recorded the many tribulations and accomplishments of his life and the decades before independence in his many books, notable among them are *'India Divided (1946)',* his autobiography *'Atmakatha (1946)'*, and *'Bapu ke Kadmon Mein (1954).'*

~

His sensitivity combined with his talents and sharp intelligence distinguished him from others. He was a man of simple living and high thinking. Endowed with outstanding qualities of head and heart he will ever remain on a high pedestal as a living legend of human values and spiritual values.

It may be said of him more truly than of anyone else that he was a perfect gentleman, the embodiment of the best in Indian life, a symbol of the good Indian. His services to the nation have already become a saga in history, of the emancipation of our country. His extreme simplicity, great humility and complete lack of ostentation marked him out as a man of the people.

References

[1] Two and a half years after Independence, on 26 January, 1950 the Constitution of independent India was ratified and he was elected the nation's first president.

[2] The Constituent Assembly took almost three years (2 years 11 months and 17 days) to complete its historic task of drafting the Constitution for independent India. During this period it held 1 sessions covering total of 165 days. Of these 114 days were spent on the consideration of the Draft Constitution.

[3] Source: Parliament Archives.

[4] On February 4, 1922 there were violent clashes between those participating in the non-cooperation movement and the police; a police station was burnt down in the village of Chauri Chaura in eastern U.P.

Dr Rajendra Prasad embodied the finer values of service, dedication and modesty. Endowed with outstanding qualities of head and heart, he shaped the destiny of this nation for about 12 years.

The human side of true progress.

THIRTEEN

Acharya Shri Tulsi

(Oct 20, 1914 – June 23, 1997)

Shri Tulsi is a celebrated 9th mendicant leader of the Śvetāmbara Terāpanth[1] sect and a socio-religious reformer. At the age of 22 he was selected to lead the sect and remained its head for over fifty seven years till he voluntarily renounced his Acharya *pad* in favour of Acharya Mahaprajna.

Acharya Tulsi was a visionary and conceived several ground-breaking programmes and schemes to uplift the mental, moral and emotional status of the society.

In the history of the religious tradition there are very few individuals of such courage and conviction who, disregarding their own comfort and convenience, lived and devoted their life to public welfare.

He realised that the hard earned independence of the country would be wasted if there was lack of morality in personal and public life. In March 1949 he launched the *Aṇuvrat*[2] movement to instil the very same idea of morality and integrity amongst the people.

He was also deeply interested in actively promoting *ahiṃsā*. He believed that although the danger of another world war may have receded, human greed and economic imperialism continue to be a cause of violence in the world. Consequently, he thought global, and launched a campaign to impart practical training in *ahiṃsā*, or non-violence. While his disciples carried his message of *ahiṃsā* to different parts of the world, he sought support of religious heads, dignitaries and opinion leaders for promoting peace and harmony in the world.

He believed that both peace and war originate in the minds of men. 'We have paid little or no attention to the question of transforming the human psyche.'

He was deeply influenced by the Jain doctrine of non-absolutism or *Anekāntavāda* or the doctrine of non-one-sidedness or a multifaceted view and nature of reality. Religion, according to him, is not merely rituals of worship, which may vary from one religion to another, but a universal code of conduct. His message was not limited to the Jain community but was addressed to the entire humanity, regardless of their faith.

He along with Muni Nath Mal (later Acharya Mahapragya) is credited with rediscovering the ancient Jain meditation technique of *Preksha dhyana*[3], a system which revolutionised the meditation techniques practised by Jain saints.

Acharya Shri Tulsi's impact on the community was due to the *Aṇuvrat* movement. There was a general feeling in the country that while focusing on material progress and doing substantial work in that direction, we were neglecting the human side of true progress.

Civilizations decline if there is a coarsening of moral fibre; if there is callousness of heart; a civilized human being must be free from greed, vanity, passion, anger.

Man is tending to become a robot, a mechanical instrument caring for nothing except his material welfare, preferring comfort to liberty, seemingly incapable of exercising his intelligence or acting responsibly, and letting politicians resort to direct action to enforce their point of view or fulfil their desires.

Such state of affairs is unfortunate, and to remedy this growing indiscipline, lack of rectitude and egotism Acharya Tulsi launched the *Aṇuvrat* movement; it was intended to impart education in moral and spiritual values and required strict adherence to the principles of good life.

We cannot say whether, as a result of this movement, the state of affairs has improved. Public spirit, commercial integrity, moral values, family life, habit of courtesy and civility and other aspects of ethical and fair behavior need to be cultivated. These cannot be achieved by preaching or by merely talking about them.

The only way in which these values can be cultivated is by imparting the essentials of our culture to the young people. These may be summarized in the three great words — *abhaya, ahiṃsā, asaṅga* — concepts which are common to all systems of religious thought.

~

Abhaya — the world in which we live is full of suffering: *lokam śoka hatam ca samastāni* — disease, old age, death. The *Upaniṣads* raise this question and asks whether there is a way out of these and believe that there is. Buddha speaks in a similar way; so does Christianity.

The *Bhagavadgītā* affirms — *anityam asukham lokam* — and argues that we can get rid of these troubles by the worship of the Divine. Thus we get the Ultimate Reality. *Brahma-jijñāsā* is the love of wisdom.

The only way of getting rid of fear of disease, old age and death, is by the conviction that there is something which redeems us from this world of time; something timeless.

The *Upaniṣads* say: *ānandaṃ brāhmaṇo vidvān nā bibheti kadācana*. The writer of the *Gītā* says: *mā śucaḥ* — be not afraid. The Buddha says that if we follow the ethical path, there will be an end of suffering.

Simply because we are afraid, it does not follow that there is something which removes our fear. Simply because we are hungry, it does not follow that there is food which will appease our hunger. The assumption of a Transcendent Reality may merely be a wish fulfilment. So it is argued that we should take an empirical survey of the world and by means of reason establish the Reality of something timeless and transcendent. Brahman is the world-ground.

A mere wish or a logical conclusion is not enough. We must have an encounter, a personal experience of the Supreme. Faith is not belief, but a state of the soul. All religious-philosophical systems believe in this. The Bodhi (Enlightenment) of the Buddha; the *Kevala Jñāna* (complete understanding or Supreme wisdom) and the *Saṃyog darśana* (right perception — to see things as they are) of the Jains; the integrated insight, the

Brahma-saṁsparśa (sharing of Brahman's vision or unity of touch, a feeling of one-in-many and many-in-one) of the *Gītā;* Truth, which casts out fear, of the Christians — these all depend on personal realization.

According to the Indian systems of thought this insight into Reality means the discovery of the Divine in us.

The *Chhāndogya Upaniṣad*[4] says that the truth by which this whole world is sustained is in the human being — *etad atmāyam idam sarvam tat satyam sa atma tat twam asi.* Again, *esa devo visvakarma matatma sada jananam hrdaye sannivistah-deho devalayo nama.*

Buddha's meditations are an endeavour to know the highest. The Jains believe that behind the body of karma, there is in each soul infinite knowledge, infinite power, infinite happiness. The *jīv* (Sanskrit: जीव — living substance or a living substance akin to soul), by its very nature, is pure. Ultimate knowledge is its inherent possession. It is overlaid by ignorance created by the karmic body. When dwelling within the bonds of karma, the *jīv* experiences only finite knowledge, but as the impediments to greater knowledge are removed, infinite knowledge is manifested and the true nature of the soul is revealed. The impediments are desires and passions.

The perfected soul is *sidha parameṣṭhin*[5]. It is a state of unconditioned being, passionless peace, dissociated from desire and action. The *arhat* (one who is worthy) has not reached ultimate liberation but works in the world with compassion for it. Then we have ordinary human teachers.

From this follows a kind of hospitality to all religious creeds.

ajo'pi sann avyayatma bhutanam isvaro'pi san prakrtim
svam adhisthaya sambhavamy atmamayaya.

Both peace and war originate in the minds of men. We have paid little or no attention to the question of transforming the human psyche.

Though (I am) unborn, my self is imperishable, though I am the Lord of all creation, yet establishing myself in my own nature, I come into (empiric[6]) being through my power.

Syadvada[7] affirms that the absolute of experience is not the absolute of language or of logic. We should not quarrel about the names we give to the Supreme or the ways by which we greet Him. On the wings of aspiration, man rises from earth to heaven, from ignorance to knowledge, from darkness to light. Without this aspiration man remains purely animal, earthly, sensual, unenlightened and uninspired.

~

Ahiṃsā — If we believe that each individual has the Divine in him, it follows that our attitude towards others should be one of non-injury. *Ahiṃsā* is *vaira tyāga* — renunciation of hatred. There is no doubt that all those who are free from fear, who have attained *abhaya* will act in a spirit of love and compassion — *karuṇā*. Love is the basis of all civilized living.

All our unhappiness is traceable to our insatiable selfishness. Suffering is the result of craving, of greed. Our life will be suffering and our end (will be full of) sorrow, until we overcome our selfishness. *Maraṇa* is not extinction. It is the extinction of craving which makes life meaningful and fulfilling. It is serenity of the soul.

Buddha says: 'To those in need give without restraint.'

Tyaga or renunciation is the way to it. Not by giving up vain clothing or outward riches, not by abstaining from certain foods, but by giving up the spirit of vanity, the desire for wealth, the lust for self-indulgence, by giving up hatred, jealousy and selfishness, do we attain purity of heart.

The man of passion is eager to put others right, the man of wisdom puts himself right. Self-conquest means self-liberation.

Triratna (the three jewels) of the Jains is right faith, right knowledge and right conduct.

The *Pañcaśīla* (or the five precepts) of the Jains is *ahiṃsā* (non-violence); *satya* (truth); *asteya* (non-stealing); *brahmacarya* (celibacy or restraint in sexual activity); and *aparigraha* (non-possesiveness) and of the Buddhists is practically the same, *ahiṃsā, satya-vacana, brahmacarya, aparigrahā* and *surā-pāṇa-niṣedha.*

~

Asaṅga — while we work in this world, we do so free from any attachment to the results of action — *yogasthaḥ kuru karmāṇi saṅgaṁ tyaktvā dhanañjaya.*

Again, *gata saṅgasya muktasya.*

Muktah is free from *saṅga.* We are unattached but not uninterested.

If we are able to spread these essentials of spiritual life, freedom from fear, love and non-attachment, we will improve the character of human beings.

~

Aṇuvrat Saṅgha which Acharya Tulsi established aims at this moral improvement of the individual and, therefore, of the society.

A true democracy has for its aim the making of moral personalities. Political power in a democracy is attained by appeals to people through the Press and other platforms. Moral power, on the other hand, resides in a moral personality and in the latter's compelling characteristic.

There is always this difference between the King and the Prophet, Rama and Vasistha, the political and the spiritual power. According to the English philosopher Thomas Hobbes[8], 'perpetual and restless desire of power that ceaseth only in death'. Its end is enslavement and its sanction force and the manipulation of society for personal greed. Spiritual leaders speak of the soul and the health of the soul; they utter words that provoke, stimulate, and awaken: they are not objects of knowledge but stimulants to thought, ungraspable but always beckoning us. These we should hold before us in all our activities.

The basic premise of *Aṇuvrat* is as relevent today as it was when it was first expounded — reform of the individual.

Collective action for propagating the ideas of *Aṇuvrat* notwithstanding, one cannot ignore its basic premise i.e. the reform of the individual. This basic premise is as relevant today as it was when it was first expounded.

Acharya Tulsi, was magnanimous in life and glorious in death. He continues to live in the hearts and minds of millions of people for whose mental, emotional, and spiritual upliftment he dedicated his life.

References

[1] Terapānth is a religious sect founded by Śvetāmbara Muni Bhikkanaji (later Acharya Bhiksu) on June 28, 1760 (Vikram Samvat 1817). His deep desire for self-purification inspired him to transcend the prevailing tradition which he believed was not in conformity with the truth and initiate this new path based entirely on Jain ideology. Terāpanth is non-idolatrous and finely organized under the complete direction of one Acharya — that is, the religious Supreme.

[2] *Aṇuvrat* movement: Aṇuvrat is a combination of two words — *aṇu* meaning small and *vrat* meaning vows. It aims to develop humane and moral conduct in people.

[3] *Preksha-dhyana*: The objective of this technique of meditation is total freedom from attachment and aversion — the two elements that distort our consciousness.

[4] *Chhāndogya Upaniṣad* is a part of the *Chhāndogya Brahmana* of the *Samveda.*

[5] *Sidha Paramesthin*:

[6] The dispute between rationalism and empiricism concerns the extent to which we are dependent upon sense experience on our effort to gain knowledge. Rationalists claim that there are significant ways in which concepts and knowledge are gained independently of sense experience. Empiricists claim that sense experience is the ultimate source of all our concepts and knowledge.

[7] *Syādvāda* is Jain metaphysics doctrine which says all judgements are conditional, holding good in certain circumstances, conditions or senses.

[8] Thomas Hobbes was the 17th century English philosopher who is considered one of the founders of modern political philosophy.

A man of profound humanism, a civilized mind free from narrow prejudices of race and language, caste and religion.

FOURTEEN

Maulana Abul Kalam Azad

(Nov 11, 1888 – Feb 22, 1958)

Maulana Abul Kalam was a towering personality in our nation's political life for nearly two generations; a man of great courage, fearlessness, integrity and passionate love for freedom.

Even before he joined the Congress in 1920, he had become a revolutionary. In 1912, while in his teens, he began publishing a weekly Urdu newspaper in Calcutta, *Al-Hilal* (The Crescent). The paper became highly influential in the Muslim community for its anti-British stance, notably for its criticism of Indian Muslims who were loyal to the British. Soon *Al-Hilal* was banned by the British authorities, as was the second weekly newspaper* that he started.

---

* *Al-Balagh.*

As a member of the Indian National Congress he galvanized the Muslim community through appeal to pan-Islamic ideals and soon emerged as an important national leader. He served as a member and general secretary of the Congress Working Committee (CWC). His political wisdom, patriotic fervour and sacrificial service were recognized early and was elected the President of the Indian National Congress in 1923 — the youngest ever — a position which he held for a number of years on different crucial occasions.

As Congress President he negotiated with Cripps[1] in 1942, with Wavell[2] in 1945, and with the Cabinet Mission[3] in 1946. As a close friend of Gandhi he was involved in various civil-disobedience campaigns, including the Salt March[4] (1930). He was imprisoned several times between 1920 and 1945, including for his participation in the Quit India movement.

In 1928, Maulana Azad endorsed the Nehru Report, formulated by Motilal Nehru. Interestingly, the Motilal Nehru Report was severely criticized by a number of Muslim personalities involved with the freedom movement. As opposed to Muhammad Ali Jinnah, Azad also advocated for the ending of separate electorates based on religion and called for a single nation committed to secularism.

After the World War II Azad was one of the few Indian leaders involved in negotiating with the British for independent India. He advocated tirelessly for a single country that would embrace both Hindus and Muslims and strongly opposed the partition of the country into India and Pakistan. Later, he held both leaders of the Congress Party and Mohammed Ali Jinnah, the founder of Pakistan, responsible for the ultimate division of the subcontinent.

After independence, he served with distinction as minister of education in the Indian government of Jawaharlal Nehru from 1947 until his death.

~

He suffered for his convictions. Among the great qualities of leadership he had was this: he never shrank from expressing his views for fear of losing popularity. A leader has to be firm. No man can be a leader if he does not risk unpopularity for his views. He who tries to please all, ends by pleasing none.

Maulana Azad noticed the shortcomings which made for subjection, and struggled to the best of his ability to remove them. National dissensions have been a frequent cause of our repeated public humiliation and subjection. He was firmly against such tendencies; he advocated oneness and consensus based progress of the country.

Though a devout Muslim whose work on the *Quran* has become a classic, he made no distinction between a Hindu or a Muslim, a Sikh and or a Christian. He felt that all those who grew up and lived in this country belonged to this country.

The national spirit was the driving force of his life. He was an apostle of national unity and communal harmony. Unity of the country cannot ever be taken for granted; there are forces which are still at work in this country to divide us from one another and such forces will always exist. That is one big learning from his life. The nation has to be nourished with delicate care, and more so in these days of linguistic and regional dissensions. Differences and diversity are the foundations of this country and enrich the unity of India.

Compassion in personal relations and justice in public affairs were Maulana Azad's principles.

He had a clear vision of what was right and what was wrong in public affairs. While he allowed compassion to sway his behaviour in personal relations, he never deviated from principles of justice so far as public affairs were concerned. He might forgive a man if he insulted him personally, but he who did a national disservice had to be dealt with adequately. Compassion in personal relations and justice in public affairs were his principles.

If we neglect probity in administration, the stability of the Government and the stability of our social structure will be undermined. He was much too fond of the right to prefer the wrong or the expedient. All along, whenever questions of administrative integrity arose, he fought for preserving high standards in public administration. That is another lesson which we have to remember.

He had strong views on the tasks before independent India. Freedom, he argued, must be used for promoting social welfare, to cleanse the country of sickness, squalor, illiteracy, and to cleanse our minds of superstition, of obscurantism, of fanaticism.

We had in Maulana Sahib a civilized mind — a mind which was free from narrow prejudices of race and language, province and dialect, caste and religion.

~

Books were his constant and unfailing companions. Whenever I went to discuss any subject with him, he always quoted from Arabic and Persian literature and wisdom to buttress his thinking. His command over both these languages was unsurpassed and also over Urdu; the speeches which he gave in Urdu were polished and firm in structure, dignified in choice of words, cogently reasoned, pointed in purpose and delivered in impeccable diction.

His work titled *Introduction to History of Philosophy, Eastern and Western*, begins with a Persian couplet which compares the universe to an old manuscript of which the first and the last pages are lost. It is no longer possible to say how the book begins nor do we know how it is likely to end.

To find out the meaning of life and existence is the purpose of philosophical quest. We may not succeed in finding it out but the pursuit of this quest is its own reward.

avyāktadīni bhūtāni vyakta-madhyāni bhārata avyakta nidhanānyeva tatra kā paridevanā.

Maulana Azad ends the introduction with another Persian couplet which says: 'Those who follow this path never tire because it is both the way and the destination.' His life is an illustration of this. It was both the search and the attainment.

~

His services to the country as a sagacious statesman, an ardent patriot, and a great intellectual are inestimable.

Let us remember that he worked for the ideals of national unity, probity in administration and economic progress. These are the things which we have to set before ourselves. The only way in which we can honour his memory is for us to adopt these ideals and question ourselves every day, whether in our acts we are promoting national unity, we are promoting integrity in administration, we are promoting economic and material progress. That is the way in which we can imbibe the lessons of his life.

There is no doubt that we will not see the like of him again — a great man of profound humanism, stately presence, indomitable courage and fearless behaviour.

References

[1] The Cripps Mission was an unsuccessful 1942 attempt by the British government to secure Indian support for World War II.

Sir John Cripps wanted a loyal India in exchange for a promise of elections and full self-government (Dominion status) after the war. Both the Congress and Muslim League rejected the proposal. Congress started the Quit India movement and refused to support the war efforts.

[2] In 1945 Lord Wavell the Viceroy of India announced the Wavell Plan — his proposals to break the constitutional deadlock in India. He invited 21 political leaders including Gandhi and Jinnah to Shimla to discuss the Plan.

Jinnah opposed the Congress nominating Muslim members to the Council and insisted that the League was the sole representative of Muslims; Congress did not agree. The conference failed and after the war a new government sent the Cabinet Mission with the intent on giving independence to India without delay.

[3] Cabinet Mission in 1946, an all-party British parliamentary delegation came to India to convince the Indian leaders of their desire for an early settlement of the Indian constitutional issue. On behalf of the Congress negotiations were conducted by Abul Kalam Azad, assisted by Nehru and Patel; negotiations got bogged down on the basic question of a united India or a divided country as the Muslim League wanted.

[4] Salt March or Dandi March was the first major Satyagraha by Gandhi against the highly repressive law prohibiting Indians from producing or distributing salt independently and forcing them to buy highly taxed imported salt. On April 6, 1930 after walking 240 miles (385 km) from Sabarmati Gandhi and his followers picked up handful of salt on the shores of Arabian Sea thus technically breaking the law prohibiting production of salt.

❑❑❑

Key for Diacritical Marks

Upaniṣada	a	=	अ	Pronounced as 'u' in cup.
Brāhman	ā	=	आ	Pronounced as 'a' in march.
Taittiriya	ai	=	ऐ	Pronounced as 'a' in cap.
Gauravāt	au	=	औ	Pronounced as 'ow' in brow.
Brahmā	b	=	ब	Pronounced as 'b' in bat.
Bhārat	bh	=	भ	Pronounced as 'bh' in Bhopal
Vācaspatī	c	=	च	Pronounced as 'ch' in church
Pucchḥai	chḥ	=	छ	Pronounced as 'chh' in Chhatisgarh.
Ātmavid	d	=	द्	Pronounced as 'th' in though.
Ādi	da	=	द	Pronounced as 'th' in the.
Ḍamru	ḍ	=	ड	Pronounced as 'd' in double.
Dharma	dh	=	ध	Pronounced as 'dh' in dhoti.
Veda	e	=	ए	Pronounced as 'e' in offend.
Granthān	g	=	ग	Pronounced as 'g' in grapes.
Ghanshyam	gh	=	घ	Pronounced as 'gh' in ghoul/ghost.
Mahāvira	h	=	ह	Pronounced as 'h' in hat.
Vidyā	i	=	इ	Pronounced as 'i' in inn.
Īśvara	ī	=	ई	Pronounced as 'ee' in creek.
Jina	j	=	ज	Pronounced as 'j' in jug.
Majjhima	jh	=	झ	Pronounced as 'jh' in Jhelum.
Jñāna	gya	=	ज्ञ	Pronounced as 'gya' in Borgia.
Akṛtaḥ	k	=	क	Pronounced as 'k' in kite.
Bhikhave	kh	=	ख	Pronounced as 'kh' in khan.
Cakṣuḥ	ḥ	=	अः	Pronounced as 'uhh' in uhh.
Lābhyo	l	=	ल	Pronounced as 'l' in lamp.

Grāhyam	m	=	म्	Pronounced as 'm' in camp.
Mantravid	ma	=	म	Pronounced as 'm' in madam.
Śaṁkara	ṁ	=	अं	Pronounced as 'ung' in clung.
Mantra	n	=	न्	Pronounced as 'n' in shrink.
Kṛtena	na	=	न	Pronounced as 'n' in nose.
Brāhmaṇa	ṇ	=	ण	Pronounced as 'ṇ' in varṇa.
Bodhi	o	=	ओ	Pronounced as 'o' in hoe.
Pratiloma	p	=	प	Pronounced as 'p' in pink.
Phalam	ph	=	फ	Pronounced as 'f' in full.
Shariq	q	=	क़	Pronounced as 'que' in oblique.
Sūtra	r	=	र्	Pronounced as 'r' in brown.
Guṇāśrayah	ra	=	र	Pronounced as 'r' in race.
Urhnā	rh	=	ड़	Pronounced as 'rh' in Rhodesia.
Muḍḥo	ḍḥ	=	ढ़	Pronounced as 'rh' in rhinoceros.
Ṛg	ṛ	=	ऋ	Pronounced as 'ri' in ring.
Yasya	s	=	स्	Pronounced as 's' in swing.
Satya	sa	=	स	Pronounced as 's' in subtle.
Śūdra	ś	=	श	Pronounced as 'sh' in shoe.
Viṣṇu	ṣ	=	ष	Pronounced as 'sh' in shingle.
Ātmā	t	=	त्	Pronounced as 't' in mitre.
Sat	ta	=	त	Pronounced as 't' in Dante.
Kuṭumbakam	ṭ	=	ट	Pronounced as 't' in cricket.
Vṛthā	th	=	थ	Pronounced as 'th' in thought.
Kaṭḥa	ṭḥ	=	ठ	Pronounced as 'ṭḥ' in Thomas.
Anuloma	u	=	उ	Pronounced as 'u' in hue.
Svarūpa	ū	=	ऊ	Pronounced as 'oo' in scooter.
Mahāvīra	v	=	व्	Pronounced as 'v' in living.
Vacana	va	=	व	Pronounced as 'v' in live.
Aparoksha	ksh	=	क्ष	Pronounced as 'ksh' in kshatriya.
Cintaya	y	=	य	Pronounced as 'y' in yacht.
Phiroza	z	=	ज़	Pronounced as 'z' in Aurangzeb.

Personal Notes

Living With a Purpose